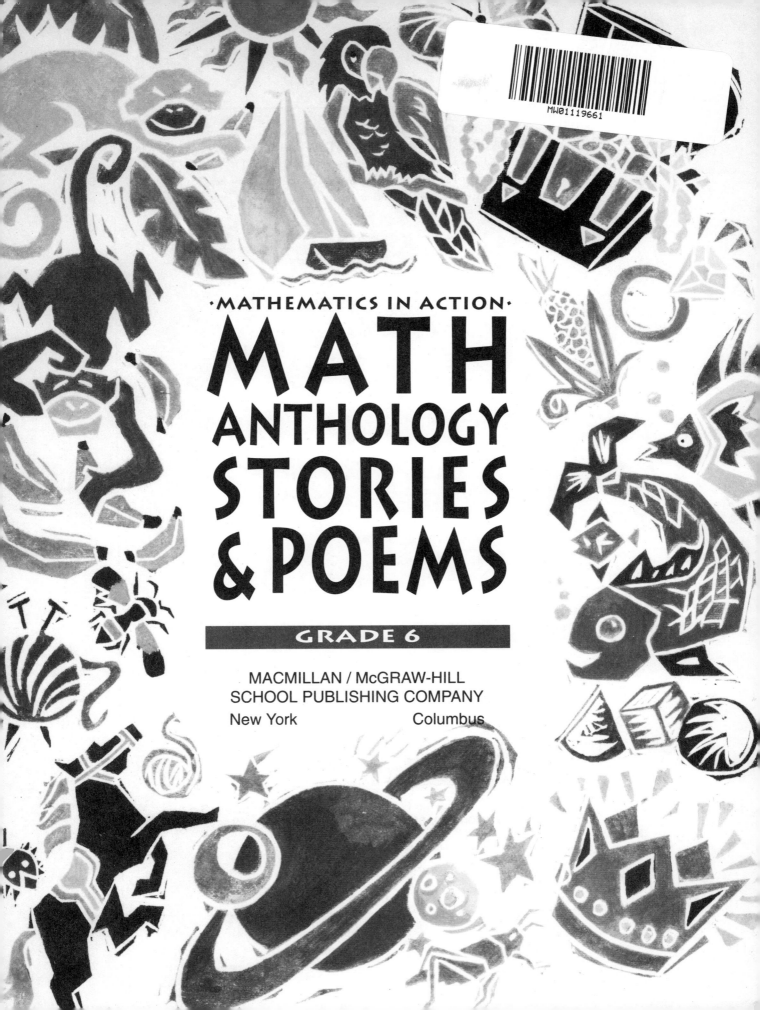

·MATHEMATICS IN ACTION·

MATH
ANTHOLOGY
STORIES
& POEMS

GRADE 6

MACMILLAN / McGRAW-HILL
SCHOOL PUBLISHING COMPANY

New York   Columbus

The **MATH ANTHOLOGY Stories and Poems** offers a variety of traditional and contemporary selections of children's literature. These selections are used as the basis for many of the individual and small-group activities in **MATHEMATICS IN ACTION**. Every story and poem is keyed to an activity in a specific lesson, and where applicable, the selections are correlated for use in other chapters.

MACMILLAN/McGRAW-HILL SCHOOL DIVISION
10 UNION SQUARE EAST, NEW YORK, NEW YORK 10003

Printed in the United States of America

ISBN 0-02-109300-8 / 6

1 2 3 4 5 6 7 8 9 BAW 99 98 97 96 95 94 93

Illustration Credits: Diane Borowski 53–54; Pat and Robin DeWitt 2–17, 25, 40, 58–64; Anne Feiza 18–19, 28, 46; Mary King 36–39, 44–45, 75; Joshua Schreier 41–43, 47–51, 55–57; Dorothea Sierra 20–21, 70–71, 72; Toni St. Regis 22–24, 73; Bea Weidner 65–69, 74

Cover Illustration: Diane Borowski

ACKNOWLEDGMENTS

The publisher gratefully acknowledges permission to reprint the following copyrighted material:

"Father and Son" from PUZZLES, PATTERNS, AND PASTIMES by Charles F. Linn. Copyright © 1969 by Charles F. Linn. Used by permission of Doubleday, a division of Bantam Doubleday Dell Publishing Group, Inc.

"Archimedes and the King's Gold Crown" by Linda Walvoord Girard from CRICKET, May 1989 issue. Reprinted by permission of Linda Walvoord Girard.

"The Passenger Pigeon" from I AM PHOENIX *Poems for Two Voices* by Paul Fleischman. Text copyright © 1985 by Paul Fleischman. Reprinted by permission of HarperCollins Publishers.

"My Knee Is Only Sprained" and "Week Before A Monday Meet:" from SPORTS PAGES by Arnold Adoff. Text copyright © 1986 by Arnold Adoff. Reprinted by permission of HarperCollins Publishers.

"Molla Nasreddin and His Donkey" from EURASIAN FOLK AND FAIRY TALES by I. F. Bulatkin. Copyright © 1965 by Criterion Books, Inc. Reprinted by permission of HarperCollins Publishers.

"Crossing the River" from STORIES TO SOLVE by George Shannon. Text copyright © 1985 by George Shannon. Reprinted by permission of Greenwillow Books, a division of William Morrow & Company, Inc.

Excerpt from EINSTEIN ANDERSON LIGHTS UP THE SKY by Seymour Simon. Copyright © 1982 by Seymour Simon. Used by permission of Viking Penguin, a division of Penguin Books USA Inc.

"Rabbinical Arithmetic" from A TREASURY OF JEWISH FOLKLORE edited by Nathan Ausubel. Copyright 1948, 1976 by Crown Publishers, Inc. Reprinted by permission of Crown Publishers, Inc.

"Shall I Consider You?" from OVERHEARD IN A BUBBLE CHAMBER AND OTHER SCIENCE POEMS by Lillian Morrison. Copyright © 1981 by Lillian Morrison. "Shall I Consider You?" first appeared in POETS ON. Reprinted by permission of Marian Reiner for the author.

"10. Be a Water-Leak Detective" from 50 SIMPLE THINGS KIDS CAN DO TO SAVE THE EARTH by The EarthWorks Group. Copyright © 1990 by John Javna. Reprinted by permission of Universal Press Syndicate. All rights reserved.

(Acknowledgments continue on page 84)

•CONTENTS•

USING THE ANTHOLOGY

This chart correlates the Anthology selections to the 1994 Grade 6 *Mathematics in Action* program. Boldface type indicates where the selection is used in the Teacher's Edition of the program.

STORIES & POEMS

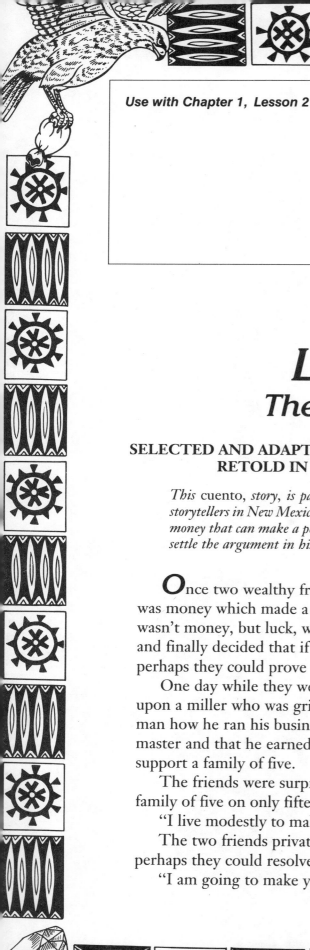

MATH CONNECTIONS

Number Sense
Addition
Subtraction
Multiplication
Division
Money

CULTURAL CONNECTION

Folktale from the Southwest

La suerte
The Force of Luck

SELECTED AND ADAPTED IN SPANISH BY JOSÉ GRIEGO Y MAESTAS
RETOLD IN ENGLISH BY RUDOLFO A. ANAYA

This cuento, *story, is part of a collection that was recorded from the original storytellers in New Mexico. Two wealthy men disagree about whether it is luck or money that can make a person successful. Each hopes a hard-working miller will settle the argument in his favor.*

Once two wealthy friends got into a heated argument. One said that it was money which made a man prosperous, and the other maintained that it wasn't money, but luck, which made the man. They argued for some time and finally decided that if only they could find an honorable man then perhaps they could prove their respective points of view.

One day while they were passing through a small village they came upon a miller who was grinding corn and wheat. They paused to ask the man how he ran his business. The miller replied that he worked for a master and that he earned only four bits a day, and with that he had to support a family of five.

The friends were surprised. "Do you mean to tell us you can maintain a family of five on only fifteen dollars a month?" one asked.

"I live modestly to make ends meet," the humble miller replied.

The two friends privately agreed that if they put this man to a test perhaps they could resolve their argument.

"I am going to make you an offer," one of them said to the miller. "I will give you two hundred dollars and you may do whatever you want with the money."

"But why would you give me this money when you've just met me?" the miller asked.

"Well, my good man, my friend and I have a long standing argument. He contends that it is luck which elevates a man to high position, and I say it is money. By giving you this money perhaps we can settle our argument. Here, take it, and do with it what you want!"

So the poor miller took the money and spent the rest of the day thinking about the strange meeting which had presented him with more money than he had ever seen. What could he possibly do with all this money? Be that as it may, he had the money in his pocket and he could do with it whatever he wanted.

When the day's work was done, the miller decided the first thing he would do would be to buy food for his family. He took out ten dollars and wrapped the rest of the money in a cloth and put the bundle in his bag. Then he went to the market and bought supplies and a good piece of meat to take home.

On the way home he was attacked by a hawk that had smelled the meat which the miller carried. The miller fought off the bird but in the struggle he lost the bundle of money. Before the miller knew what was happening the hawk grabbed the bag and flew away with it. When he realized what had happened he fell into deep thought.

"Ah," he moaned, "wouldn't it have been better to let that hungry bird have the meat! I could have bought a lot more meat with the money he took. Alas, now I'm in the same poverty as before! And worse, because now those two men will say I am a thief! I should have thought carefully and bought nothing. Yes, I should have gone straight home and this wouldn't have happened!"

So he gathered what was left of his provisions and continued home, and when he arrived he told his family the entire story.

When he was finished telling his story his wife said, "It has been our lot to be poor, but have faith in God and maybe someday our luck will change."

The next day the miller got up and went to work as usual. He wondered what the two men would say about his story. But since he had never been a man of money he soon forgot the entire matter.

Three months after he had lost the money to the hawk, it happened that the two wealthy men returned to the village. As soon as they saw the miller they approached him to ask if his luck had changed. When the miller saw them he felt ashamed and afraid that they would think that he had squandered the money on worthless things. But he decided to tell them the truth and as soon as they had greeted each other he told his story. The men believed him. In fact, the one who insisted that it was money and not luck which made a man prosper took out another two hundred dollars and gave it to the miller.

"Let's try again," he said, "and let's see what happens this time."

The miller didn't know what to think. "Kind sir, maybe it would be better if you put this money in the hands of another man," he said.

"No," the man insisted, "I want to give it to you because you are an honest man, and if we are going to settle our argument you have to take the money!"

The miller thanked them and promised to do his best. Then as soon as the two men left he began to think what to do with the money so that it wouldn't disappear as it had the first time. The thing to do was to take the money straight home. He took out ten dollars, wrapped the rest in a cloth, and headed home.

When he arrived his wife wasn't at home. At first he didn't know what to do with the money. He went to the pantry where he had stored a large earthenware jar filled with bran. That was as safe a place as any to hide the money, he thought, so he emptied out the grain and put the bundle of money at the bottom of the jar and covered it up with the grain. Satisfied that the money was safe he returned to work.

That afternoon when he arrived home from work he was greeted by his wife.

"Look, my husband, today I bought some good clay with which to whitewash the entire house."

"And how did you buy the clay if we don't have any money?" he asked.

"Well, the man who was selling the clay was willing to trade for jewelry, money, or anything of value," she said. "The only thing we had of value was the jar full of bran, so I traded it for the clay. Isn't it wonderful, I think we have enough clay to whitewash these two rooms!"

The man groaned and pulled his hair.

"Oh, you crazy woman! What have you done? We're ruined again!"

"But why?" she asked, unable to understand his anguish.

"Today I met the same two friends who gave me the two hundred dollars three months ago," he explained. "And after I told them how I lost the money they gave me another two hundred. And I, to make sure the money was safe, came home and hid it inside the jar of bran — the same jar you have traded for dirt! Now we're as poor as we were before! And what am I going to tell the two men? They'll think I'm a liar and a thief for sure!"

"Let them think what they want," his wife said calmly. "We will only have in our lives what the good Lord wants us to have. It is our lot to be poor until God wills it otherwise."

So the miller was consoled and the next day he went to work as usual. Time came and went, and one day the two wealthy friends returned to ask the miller how he had done with the second two hundred dollars. When the poor miller saw them he was afraid they would accuse him of being a liar and a spendthrift. But he decided to be truthful and as soon as they had greeted each other he told them what had happened to the money.

"That is why poor men remain honest," the man who had given him the money said. "Because they don't have money they can't get into trouble. But I find your stories hard to believe. I think you gambled and lost the money. That's why you're telling us these wild stories."

"Either way," he continued, "I still believe that it is money and not luck which makes a man prosper."

"Well, you certainly didn't prove your point by giving the money to this poor miller," his friend reminded him. "Good evening, you luckless man," he said to the miller.

"Thank you, friends," the miller said.

"Oh, by the way, here is a worthless piece of lead I've been carrying around. Maybe you can use it for something," said the man who believed in luck. Then the two men left, still debating their points of view on life.

Since the lead was practically worthless, the miller thought nothing of it and put it in his jacket pocket. He forgot all about it until he arrived home. When he threw his jacket on a chair he heard a thump and he remembered the piece of lead. He took it out of the pocket and threw it under the table. Later that night after the family had eaten and gone to bed, they heard a knock at the door.

"Who is it? What do you want?" the miller asked.

"It's me, your neighbor," a voice answered. The miller recognized the fisherman's wife. "My husband sent me to ask you if you have any lead you can spare. He is going fishing tomorrow and he needs the lead to weight down the nets."

The miller remembered the lead he had thrown under the table. He got up, found it, and gave it to the woman.

"Thank you very much, neighbor," the woman said. "I promise you the first fish my husband catches will be yours."

"Think nothing of it," the miller said and returned to bed. The next day he got up and went to work without thinking any more of the incident. But in the afternoon when he returned home he found his wife cooking a big fish for dinner.

"Since when are we so well off we can afford fish for supper?" he asked his wife.

"Don't you remember that our neighbor promised us the first fish her husband caught?" his wife reminded him. "Well this was the fish he caught the first time he threw his net. So it's ours, and it's a beauty. But you should have been here when I gutted him! I found a large piece of glass in his stomach!"

"And what did you do with it?"

"Oh, I gave it to the children to play with," she shrugged.

When the miller saw the piece of glass he noticed it shone so brightly it appeared to illuminate the room, but because he knew nothing about jewels he didn't realize its value and left it to the children. But the bright glass was such a novelty that the children were soon fighting over it and raising a terrible fuss.

Now it so happened that the miller and his wife had other neighbors who were jewelers. The following morning when the miller had gone to work the jeweler's wife visited the miller's wife to complain about all the noise her children had made.

"We couldn't get any sleep last night," she moaned.

"I know, and I'm sorry, but you know how it is with a large family," the miller's wife explained. "Yesterday we found a beautiful piece of glass and I gave it to my youngest one to play with and when the others tried to take it from him he raised a storm."

The jeweler's wife took interest. "Won't you show me that piece of glass?" she asked.

"But of course. Here it is."

"Ah, yes, it's a pretty piece of glass. Where did you find it?"

"Our neighbor gave us a fish yesterday and when I was cleaning it I found the glass in its stomach."

"Why don't you let me take it home for just a moment. You see, I have one just like it and I want to compare them."

"Yes, why not? Take it," answered the miller's wife.

So the jeweler's wife ran off with the glass to show it to her husband. When the jeweler saw the glass he instantly knew it was one of the finest diamonds he had ever seen.

"It's a diamond!" he exclaimed.

"I thought so," his wife nodded eagerly. "What shall we do?"

"Go tell the neighbor we'll give her fifty dollars for it, but don't tell her it's a diamond!"

"No, no," his wife chuckled, "of course not." She ran to her neighbor's house. "Ah yes, we have one exactly like this," she told the miller's wife. "My husband is willing to buy it for fifty dollars — only so we can have a pair, you understand."

"I can't sell it," the miller's wife answered. "You will have to wait until my husband returns from work."

That evening when the miller came home from work his wife told him about the offer the jeweler had made for the piece of glass.

"But why would they offer fifty dollars for a worthless piece of glass?" the miller wondered aloud. Before his wife could answer they were interrupted by the jeweler's wife.

"What do you say, neighbor, will you take fifty dollars for the glass?" she asked.

"No, that's not enough," the miller said cautiously. "Offer more."

"I'll give you fifty thousand!" the jeweler's wife blurted out.

"A little bit more," the miller replied.

"Impossible!" the jeweler's wife cried, "I can't offer any more without consulting my husband." She ran off to tell her husband how the bartering was going, and he told her he was prepared to pay a hundred thousand dollars to acquire the diamond.

He handed her seventy-five thousand dollars and said, "Take this and tell him that tomorrow, as soon as I open my shop, he'll have the rest."

When the miller heard the offer and saw the money he couldn't believe his eyes. He imagined the jeweler's wife was jesting with him, but it was a true offer and he received the hundred thousand dollars for the diamond. The miller had never seen so much money but he still didn't quite trust the jeweler.

"I don't know about this money," he confided to his wife.

"Maybe the jeweler plans to accuse us of robbing him and thus get it back."

"Oh no," his wife assured him, "the money is ours. We sold the diamond fair and square—we didn't rob anyone."

"I think I'll still go to work tomorrow," the miller said. "Who knows, something might happen and the money will disappear, then we would be without money and work. Then how would we live?"

So he went to work the next day, and all day he thought about how he could use the money. When he returned home that afternoon his wife asked him what he had decided to do with their new fortune.

"I think I will start my own mill," he answered, "like the one I operate for my master. Once I set up my business we'll see how our luck changes."

The next day he set about buying everything he needed to establish his mill and to build a new home. Soon he had everything going.

Six months had passed, more or less, since he had seen the two men who had given him the four hundred dollars and the piece of lead. He was eager to see them again and to tell them how the piece of lead had changed his luck and made him wealthy.

Time passed and the miller prospered. His business grew and he even built a summer cottage where he could take his family on vacation. He had many employees who worked for him. One day while he was at his store he saw his two benefactors riding by. He rushed out into the street to greet them and ask them to come in. He was overjoyed to see them, and he was happy to see that they admired his store.

"Tell us the truth," the man who had given him the four hundred dollars said. "You used that money to set up this business."

The miller swore he hadn't, and he told them how he had given the piece of lead to his neighbor and how the fisherman had in return given him a fish with a very large diamond in its stomach. And he told them how he had sold the diamond.

"And that's how I acquired this business and many other things I want to show you," he said. "But it's time to eat. Let's eat first then I'll show you everything I have now."

The men agreed, but one of them still doubted the miller's story. So they ate and then the miller had three horses saddled and they rode out to see his summer home. The cabin was on the other side of the river where the mountains were cool and beautiful. When they arrived the men admired the place very much. It was such a peaceful place that they rode all afternoon through the forest. During their ride they came upon a tall pine tree.

"What is that on top of the tree?" one of them asked.

"That's the nest of a hawk," the miller replied.

"I have never seen one; I would like to take a closer look at it!"

"Of course," the miller said, and he ordered a servant to climb the tree and bring down the nest so his friend could see how it was built. When the hawk's nest was on the ground they examined it carefully. They noticed that there was a cloth bag at the bottom of the nest. When the miller saw the bag he immediately knew that it was the very same bag he had lost to the hawk which fought him for the piece of meat years ago.

"You won't believe me, friends, but this is the very same bag in which I put the first two hundred dollars you gave me," he told them.

"If it's the same bag," the man who had doubted him said, "then the money you said the hawk took should be there."

"No doubt about that," the miller said. "Let's see what we find."

The three of them examined the old, weatherbeaten bag. Although it was full of holes and crumbling, when they tore it apart they found the money intact. The two men remembered what the miller had told them and they agreed he was an honest and honorable man. Still, the man who had given him the money wasn't satisfied. He wondered what had really happened to the second two hundred he had given the miller.

They spent the rest of the day riding in the mountains and returned very late to the house.

As he unsaddled their horses, the servant in charge of grooming and feeding the horses suddenly realized that he had no grain for them. He ran to the barn and checked, but there was no grain for the hungry horses. So he ran to the neighbor's granary and there he was able to buy a large clay jar of bran. He carried the jar home and emptied the bran into a bucket to wet it before he fed it to the horses. When he got to the bottom of the jar he noticed a large lump which turned out to be a rag covered package. He examined it and felt something inside. He immediately went to give it to his master who had been eating dinner.

"Master," he said, "look at this package which I found in an earthenware jar of grain which I just bought from our neighbor!"

The three men carefully unraveled the cloth and found the other one hundred and ninety dollars which the miller had told them he had lost. That is how the miller proved to his friends that he was truly an honest man.

And they had to decide for themselves whether it had been luck or money which had made the miller a wealthy man!

La suerte
The Force of Luck

*E*stos eran dos compañeros que andaban en una porfía, uno decía que el dinero levantaba al hombre y el otro sostenía que no era el dinero, sino la suerte. Aunduvieron porfiando mucho tiempo con deseos de encontrar un hombre honrado para poder probar sus puntos de vista.

Tocó la casualidad un día que pasando por una plaza se encontraron con un molinero que estaba moliendo maíz y trigo. Se dirigieron a donde estaba el hombre para preguntarle cómo corria su negocio. El hombre les respondió muy atentamente que él trabajaba por otro señor y que ganaba solamente cuatro reales al día, con lo que mantenía a su familia de cinco.

"Y usted, ¿se acabala con quince pesos al mes para mantener a su familia de cinco?"

"Pues me limito todo lo que puedo para mantener a mi familia, no porque tengo suficiente."

"Pues entonces le voy a hacer un presente. Aquí le voy a regalar doscientos pesos para ver lo que va a determinar hacer con ellos."

"No, señor" le dijo el hombre, "no creo que usted me pueda regalar ese dinero la primera vez que yo lo miro a usted."

"Señor" le dijo él, "yo le voy a dejar este dinero a usted porque yo y este hombre porfiamos. El porfía que la suerte es la que levanta al hombre y yo dingo que el dinero es el que levanta."

Cuando el hombre pobre tomó el dinero, pasó todo el día relfexionando sobre aquel negocio. ¿Qué podría hacer con todo el dinero? Aquel hombre se lo dio para calarlo, y él podría determinar del dinero como si fuera suyo. Sea como fuere, él tenía el dinero en su bolsa e iba a determinar de ello como le pareciere.

Se llegó la hora de salir del trabajo y se fue él con su dinero a comprar algunas provisiones para su familia. Tomó diez pesos y envolvió los ciento noventa restantes en unos trapos y en una blusa de lona que traiba. Cuando llegó a la plaza, trató bastantes negocios allí y compró un buen pedazo de carne para llevarle a su familia.

En el camino a su casa, al olor de la carne, le salió un gavilán hambriento. El hombre se puso a pelear con el gavilán; el animal andaba

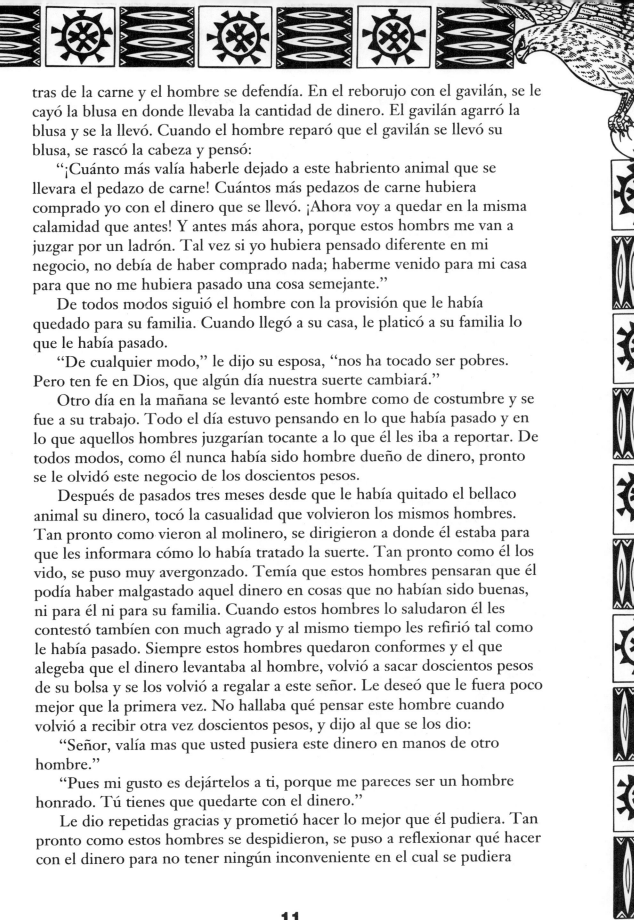

tras de la carne y el hombre se defendía. En el reborujo con el gavilán, se le cayó la blusa en donde llevaba la cantidad de dinero. El gavilán agarró la blusa y se la llevó. Cuando el hombre reparó que el gavilán se llevó su blusa, se rascó la cabeza y pensó:

"¡Cuánto más valía haberle dejado a este habriento animal que se llevara el pedazo de carne! Cuántos más pedazos de carne hubiera comprado yo con el dinero que se llevó. ¡Ahora voy a quedar en la misma calamidad que antes! Y antes más ahora, porque estos hombrs me van a juzgar por un ladrón. Tal vez si yo hubiera pensado diferente en mi negocio, no debía de haber comprado nada; haberme venido para mi casa para que no me hubiera pasado una cosa semejante."

De todos modos siguió el hombre con la provisión que le había quedado para su familia. Cuando llegó a su casa, le platicó a su familia lo que le había pasado.

"De cualquier modo," le dijo su esposa, "nos ha tocado ser pobres. Pero ten fe en Dios, que algún día nuestra suerte cambiará."

Otro día en la mañana se levantó este hombre como de costumbre y se fue a su trabajo. Todo el día estuvo pensando en lo que había pasado y en lo que aquellos hombres juzgarían tocante a lo que él les iba a reportar. De todos modos, como él nunca había sido hombre dueño de dinero, pronto se le olvidó este negocio de los doscientos pesos.

Después de pasados tres meses desde que le había quitado el bellaco animal su dinero, tocó la casualidad que volvieron los mismos hombres. Tan pronto como vieron al molinero, se dirigieron a donde él estaba para que les informara cómo lo había tratado la suerte. Tan pronto como él los vido, se puso muy avergonzado. Temía que estos hombres pensaran que él podía haber malgastado aquel dinero en cosas que no habían sido buenas, ni para él ni para su familia. Cuando estos hombres lo saludaron él les contestó tambíen con much agrado y al mismo tiempo les refirió tal como le había pasado. Siempre estos hombres quedaron conformes y el que alegeba que el dinero levantaba al hombre, volvió a sacar doscientos pesos de su bolsa y se los volvió a regalar a este señor. Le deseó que le fuera poco mejor que la primera vez. No hallaba qué pensar este hombre cuando volvió a recibir otra vez doscientos pesos, y dijo al que se los dio:

"Señor, valía mas que usted pusiera este dinero en manos de otro hombre."

"Pues mi gusto es dejártelos a ti, porque me pareces ser un hombre honrado. Tú tienes que quedarte con el dinero."

Le dio repetidas gracias y prometió hacer lo mejor que él pudiera. Tan pronto como estos hombres se despidieron, se puso a reflexionar qué hacer con el dinero para no tener ningún inconveniente en el cual se pudiera

desperdiciar sin haberlo usado. Pensó immediatamente ir a llevar el dinero a su propia casa. Tomó diez pesos y envolvió ciento noventa en unos trapos y se fue para su casa.

Cuando llegó a su casa no encontró a su esposa. Viendo que la casa estaba sola no hallaba dónde poner el dinero. Se fue a la despensa donde tenían una tinaja lena de salvado, vació el salvado de la tinaja y puso el dinero al fondo de la tinaja envuelto ta como estaba y volvió a echar el salvado arriba del dinero. Se salió apresuradamente a su trabajo sin haberle dado cuenta a nadia.

Cuando vino en la tarde de su trabajo, su esposa le dijo:

"¡Mira, hijo! Yo compré una poca de tierra para enjarrar la casa por dentro."

"Y ¿con qué has mercado tierra, si no tenemos dinero?"

"Sí," le dice la mujer, "pero este hombre andaba vendiendo la tierra, fuera por prendas, dinero, o cualquiera cosa. La única cosa de valor que teníamos para feriar era la tinaja de salvado, así que le di la tinaja de salvado por la tierra. Creo que será suficiente para que yo enjarre estos dos cuartos."

Se jaló de los cabellos el hombre y le interrumpió a la mujer:

"¡Ay, mujer bárbara! ¿Qué has hecho? ¡Otra vez nos quedamos en la ruina! Habías de haber visto que hoy mismo me encontré con los mismos amigos que me habían dado los doscientos pesos tres meses pasados y, habiéndoles platicado cómo perdí el dinero, me volvieron a regalar doscientos pesos más, y yo, por tenerlos más seguros, los eché dentro de la olla del salvado, ¿Qué es lo que voy a reportarle a estos hombres ahoa? Ahora acabarán de juzgar que yo soy un ladrón."

"Que piensen como quieran," dijo la mujer "que al cabo uno no tiene más que lo que Dios quiere. Ya nos tocó ser pobres. Sólo Dios sabrá hasta cuándo."

Otro día en la mañana se levantó como de costumbre y se fue a su trabajo.

Yendo y viniendo el tiempo volvieron estos hombres a donde estaba el molinero en su negocio para informarse de lo que le había pasado esta segunda vez con el dinero. Cuando el pobre los vido venir a donde estaba él, no dejó de avergonzarse y creer que estos hombres juzgaban que él era un traidor y que estaba malgastando el dinero. Tan pronto como llegaron a donde estaba él, se saludaron, y el molinero trató de hacerles saber lo que le había pasado esta vez con el segundo dinero que le habían presentado. El hombre que le había dado el dinero se sintió mal y le dijo que asina eran muchos hombres pobres, que eran muy honestos y muy honrados solamente porque no tenían dinero para andar en otras bromas. Pero como él había recibido dinero, probablemente se había dedicado a juegos, y asina es como había gastado el dinero y ahora le salía con ese cuento.

"Sea como sea," dijo el hombre, "yo todavía sostengo que los hombres se levantan a fuerza de dinero y no por la suerte."

"Bueno, entonces pase usted may buenas tardes."

"Muy bien, amigo."

"Tenga, aquí está un pedazo de plomo. Pueda que para alguna cosa le sirva," le dijo el que sostenía que la suerte era la que levantaba a los hombres y no el dinero.

Como ésta no era una cosa de valor, la recibió y se la echó en la bolsa de su chaqueta. En la tarde cuando llegó a su casa, tiró su chaqueta arriba de una silleta y oyó alguna cosa sonar. Se acordó del padazo de plomo que le había regalado este individuo, lo sacó de la bolsa y lo tiró asina como para abajo de una mesa. No volvió a hacer más recuerdo del pedazo de plomo. Cenaron él y toda su familia. Después de que cenaron, se acostaron. No más en cuanto se acabaron de acostar, sonaron la puerta.

"¿Quién es? ¿Qué se ofrece?"

"Yo, vecino. Dice su vecino que si no tiene un pedazo de plomo por ahí guardado por casualidad. Que le haga favor, si tiene, de darle un poco, que mañana tiene que hacer una pesca muy grande y no tiene suficiente plomo para componer sus redes."

En eso se acordó el hombre de que había tirado el pedazo de plomo para abajo de la mesa. Se levantó y lo buscó y se lo entregó a la mujer.

"Muy bien, vecino, muchísimas gracias. Le prometo que el primer pescado que pesque su vecino, ha de ser para usted."

Se levantó muy de mañana el hombre y se fue a su trabajo sin haber reflexionado más sobre el pedazo de plomo.

En la tarde cuando vino a la casa, encontró que tenían un pescado muy grande para cenar.

"¿De dónde, hija, estamos tan bien nosotros que vamos a cenar pescado?"

"¿No te acuerdas que anoche nos prometió la vecina que el primer pescado que pescara el vecino no lo iba a regalar a nosotros? Este fue el único pescado que pescó en la primera vez que echó la red. ¡Y si vieras hijo! ¡Lo que más me almira, que este pescado tenía adentro un pedazo de vidrio muy grande!"

"Y ¿qué hiciste con él?"

"Se lo di a los muchachos para que jugaran con él."

Fueron a ver el pedazo de vidrio que tenían los muchachitos. El vidrio iluminaba el cuarto obscuro. El hombre y la mujer no sabían lo que eran diamantes, así que no se fijaron en guardar el vidrio, sino que se lo dejaron a los muchachos para que jugaran con él. Por la novedad del vidrio los muchachos empezaron a pelear por él. Los más grandes se lo quitaban al más chiquito, por donde el chiquito hacía una bulla terrible.

Estos pobres tenían unos vecinos judíos que eran joyeros. En la mañana se levantó el hombre y se fue al trabajo. La mujer del joyero llegó después para pedirle a la mujer del molinero que tuviera más cuidado de su familia porque estaban haciendo mucha bulla los niños, y no los dejaban dormir.

"Sí, vecina es verdad lo que usted dice. Pero ya ve cómo es donde hay familia. Pues usted verá que ayer hallamos un vidrio y se lo di al niño más chiquito para que jugara con él y cuando los más grandes se lo quieren quitar, él forma un escándalo grande."

"¡A ver!" le dijo la mujer. "¿Por qué no me enseña ese vidrio?"

"Sí se lo puedo enseñar. Aquí está."

"Qué bonito vidrio es éste. ¿Dónde lo hallaron?"

"Pues adentro de un pescado. Ayer estaba limpiando un pescado y el vidrio estaba adentro de él."

"Empréstemelo para llevarlo a mi casa para ver si se parece a uno que tengo."

"Sí," le dice. "¿Por qué no?" Llévelo."

Se llevó la vecina el vidrio a enseñárselo al marido. Cuando el joyero miró este vidrio, vido que era de los diamantes más finos que jamás había visto.

"Este es un diamante," le dice a su esposa. "Anda, dile a la vecina que le damos cincuenta pesos por él."

Fue la esposa del joyero con el vidrio en la mano y le dice a la vecina:

"Dice su vecino que si quiere, que le damos cincuenta pesos por este vidrio. Todo lo hacemos porque es muy parecido a otro que tenemos nosotros y asina podíamos hacer un par muy bonito."

"De ningún modo, vecina, puedo yo vendérselo. Eso puede hacerse a la tarde cuando venga mi esposo."

En la tarde cuando vino el molinero del trabajo, le contó su esposa lo que había ofrecido su vecino el joyero. En esto estaban hablando cuando entró la mujer del joyero.

"¿Qué dice, vecino, quiere cincuenta pesos por el vidrio?"

"Alárguese poco más."

"Le daré cincuenta mil pesos."

"Poco más." le dice.

"No puedo alargarme más. Voy a ver a mi esposo a ver qué me dice. Hasta ahí no más me dijo que me alargara."

Fue la esposa del joyero y le dijo a su esposo lo que había reportado el vecino. El joyero entonces sacó setenta y cinco mil pesos y le dijo:

"Llévale estos y dile que mañana, luego que se abra allá, le traeré lo restante, que le voy a dar cien mil pesos."

Cuando el molinero vido a la mujer con aquel dineral, cuasi no lo creía él. Creía que aquella mujer estaba chanceándose. Pero sea como fuere, el pobre recibió cien mil pesos por el diamante.

Cuando el molinero se vido con tanto dinero, él y su esposa no hallaban qué pensar. Decía él:

"Pues no sé de este dinero; el joyero de repente nos podía levantar un crimen que nosotros lo hemos robado, o de alguna manera nos podía levantar u perjuicio muy grande."

"¡Oh, no!" decía la mujer. "Ese dinero es de nosotros. Nosotros vendimos el vidrio por ese dinero. Nosotros no se lo robamos a nadien."

"De todos modos yo voy mañana a trabajar, hija. No nos vaya a suceder que se nos acabe el dinero y no tengamos ni el dinero ni el trabajo y entonces, ¿cómo nos vamos a mantener?"

Se fue el hombre al otro día a su trabajo. Todo el día se estuvo pensando y pensando cómo podía dirigir aquel dinero para que le cambiara su suerte. En la tarde cuando volvió del trabajo, le dijo su esposa:

"Qué has dicho o qué has pensado? ¿Qué vas a determinar hacer con este dineral que tenemos?"

"Voy a ver si puedo poner un molino, tal como el que yo estoy corriendo de mi amo. Quiero poner un comercio y asina, poco a poco, veremos si cambiamos nuestra suerte."

Otro día este hombre se fue con mucho empeño y anduvo negociando, comprando todo lo necessario para poner un molino, un comercio, y una casa. Pronto arregló todo.

Ya pasaban como unos seis meses, tal vez más desde que no había visto a los hombres que le regalaron los cuatrocientos pesos y el pedazo de plomo. El tenía muchos deseos de verlos, para hacerles saber cuánto le había ayudado aquel pedazo de plomo que le regaló el hombre que reclamaba que la suerte era la que ayudaba al hombre a levantarse y no el dinero.

Yendo y viniendo el tiempo, el molinero estaba muy bien puesto. Tenía muy buen comercio, había levantado una casa de campo adonde irse a divertir con su familia, y tenía criados que trabajaban por él.

Un día que estaba en su tienda, vio pasar aquellos dos señores que más antes le habían regalado cuatrocientos pesos y el pedazo de plomo. Tan pronto como los vido, salió a la calle a encontrarlos y a suplicarles que le hicieran el favor de entrar para dentro. El tenía mucho de hablar con ellos y verlos. Tan pronto como entraron, aquellos hombres quedaron admirados de ver aquella tienda tan grande que él tenía. Al mismo tiempo el que le había regalado los cuatrocientos pesos no dejaba de juzgar que éste hombre había empleado aquel dinero en este comercio, pera a él se lo negaba. El molinero les platicó cómo había dado el pedazo de plomo a su vecino y luego cómo el pescador le había regalado un pescado que tenía adentro un diamante muy grande. Les contó también de la venta del diamante por una cantidad de dinero enorme y terminó diciéndoles:

"Y asina es como he adquirido este comercio y muchas otras cosas que quiero enseñarles. Pero ya es hora de comer. Vamos a tomar la comida y luego vamos a tomar un paseo para enseñarles todo lo que tengo."

Tomaron la comida y luego que acabaron de comer mandó a un muchacho que ensillara tres caballos, y se fueron los tres a pasearse para enseñarles la casa de campo que tenía. Esta casa de campo estaba al otro lado del río donde había bastante monte en un lugar muy bonito. Cuando llegaron allá, les gustó mucho el lugar a los hombres y empezaron a pasearse entre el monte. Durante su paseo le llamó la atención a uno de los hombres un nido de gavilán que estaba allá arriba en un pinabete.

"Y eso que se ve allá arriba, ¿qué cosa es?"

"Eso es un nido de gavilán," dijo el dueño del rancho.

"¡Cómo desearía ver yo ese nido más cerquita!"

En eso mandó el hombre a uno de sus criados que subiera arriba del pinabete y bajara el nido con cuidado para satisfacerle a su amigo el deseo que tenía de ver aquel nido más cerquita. Cuando el nido estaba abajo lo estuvieron examinando los tres hombres muy bien y entonces notaron que abajo del nido estaba como una blusa de lona. Cuando el molinero vido la blusa, de una vez reflexionó que era la lona que él traiba puesta cuando el gavilán habriento había peleado con él por el pedazo de carne, y no habiéndole podido quitar la carne, se había llevado la blusa entre las uñas.

"¿Qué no les parece, amigos que esta es la blusa que tenía yo el día que me regalaron los primeros doscientos pesos?"

"Pues si es esta la misma blusa," dijo él," que tenías cuando te regalamos el dinero, aquí han de estar los doscientos que tú nos reportaste que el gavilán se había robado con todo y blusa."

"Pues creo que no hay duda. Esta es mi blusa y vamos a examinar a ver qué es lo que hallamos."

Emperzaron entre los tres amigos a examinar la blusa. Aunque la blusa tenía bastantes agujeros por estar apolillada, encontraron que el lugar donde había puesto el dinero no había sido afectado de ningún modo, y el dinero estaba, perfectamente tal como él había reportado. Los dos hombres confesaron lo que el molinero les había dicho más antes y juzagaron que era un hombre honesto y honrado. Pero el hombre que le había hecho los presentes de dinero no quedaba muy satisfecho porque no había encontrado los otros ciento noventa que faltaban.

Pasaron el día muy contentos, paseándose, y ya se vinieron poco tarde a la casa. El hombre que atendía a los caballos no se había dado cuenta de que no había grano para los caballos cuando volvieran. Y en eso que llegaron, fue al comercio de ellos mismos y no encontró grano para darles a los caballos que habían llegado. Se fue a otro comercio que estaba inmediato y allá encontró que no había más que un tinaja de salvado. Trujo la tinaja de salvado y cuando llegó a la casa de su amo vació el salvado en otra cubeta para mojarlo y dárselo a los caballos. Al vaciar la tinaja notó que estaba un bulto algo grande como un empaque envuelto en unos trapos en el fondo de la tinaja. Lo cogió, lo examinó y vido que alguna cosa contenía. Hizo por quitarle bien el salvado para que quedara limpio y fue a presentarlo a su amo que estaba cenando.

"Mi señor, mire qué bulto he encontrado dentro de una tinaja que he comprado al otro comerciante."

"¿Qué es lo que hablas de tinaja?"

"Sí," le dijo, "que he hallado este envoltorio dentro de una tinaja llena de salvado."

Lo tomaron y los tres hombres allí mismo curiosamente estuvieron desenvolviendo con muy buen cuidado los trapos y descubrieron que allí estaban los otros ciento noventa que el molinero les había dicho que había perdido. Y aquí acabó de probar el molinero a sus amigos que él había tratado siempre con la verdad y que él no estaba mintiéndoles.

Y se pusieron a reflejar si era el dinero o la suerte lo que le ayudó al molinero levantarse.

The Passenger Pigeon

BY PAUL FLEISCHMAN

This poem about the extinction of the passenger pigeon should be read aloud by two readers at the same time. One reader takes the left-hand part and the other takes the right-hand part. Read from top to bottom, the lines that appear on the same horizontal level are spoken by both readers as a duet.

We were counted not in

               thousands

nor

               millions

but in

billions.   *billions.*

               We were numerous as the

stars   stars

               in the heavens.

As grains of

sand   sand

at the sea

               As the

buffalo   buffalo

               on the plains.

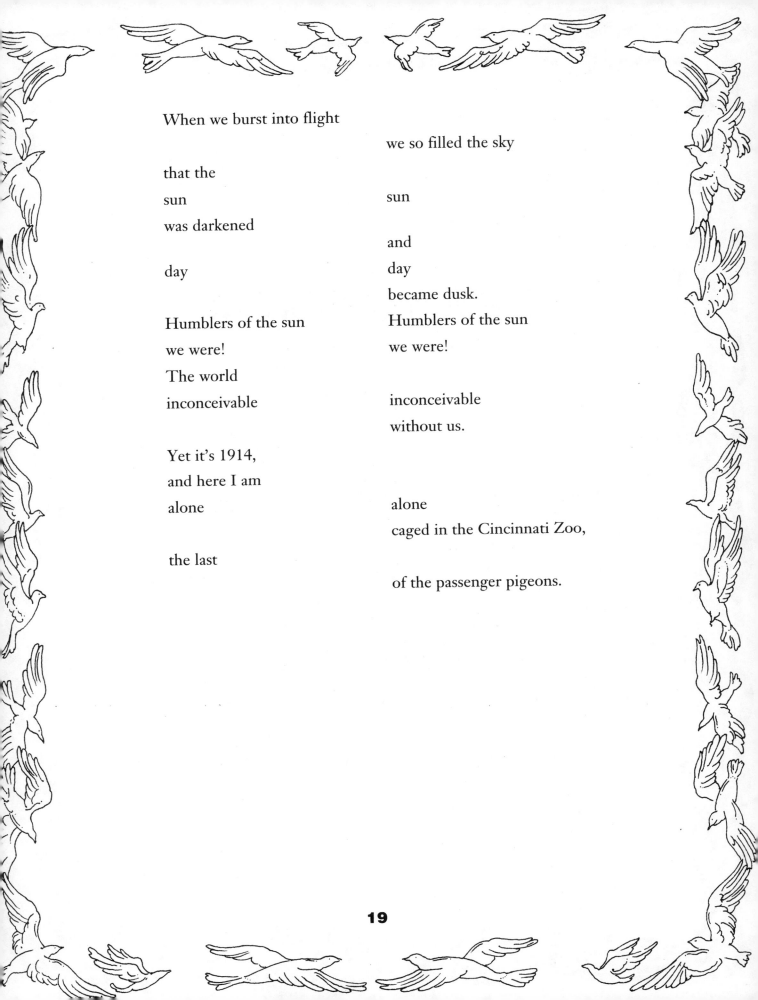

When we burst into flight

we so filled the sky

that the
sun
was darkened

sun

and
day

day
became dusk.

Humblers of the sun
we were!
The world
inconceivable

Humblers of the sun
we were!

inconceivable
without us.

Yet it's 1914,
and here I am
alone

alone
caged in the Cincinnati Zoo,

the last

of the passenger pigeons.

Be a Water-Leak Detective

FROM 50 Simple Things Kids Can Do to Save the Earth
BY THE EARTHWORKS GROUP

Take a Guess.
*If a leaky faucet fills a coffee cup in 10 minutes,
how much water will it waste in a year? Enough for:
A) A glass of water B) A bath C) 52 baths*

Calling all kids! Calling all kids! Be on the lookout for hidden water leaks in your house. Secret hiding places include: behind the walls, in faucets, in toilets . . . and even outside at the end of a hose.

Your mission as a water-leak detective is to find the hidden leaks . . . and help to stop them!

Did You Know
• Even a tiny leak can waste a lot of water. For example, a leak that fills up a coffee cup in 10 minutes will waste over 3,000 gallons of water in a year.
• How much water is that? You'd have to drink 65 glasses of water every day *for a year* to get that much water!
• 20% of all the toilets in American homes are leaking right now. . . . And usually people don't even know it.
• In one year, a leaky toilet can waste over 22,000 gallons of water. That's enough to take three baths every day!

What You Can Do
Be a Water-Leak Detective. Here's how:
• First, get your parent to teach you how to read the water meter. If you have one, it will probably be in the corner of your basement, on the outside wall of your house, or next to the street, under a cement or metal cover.
• Then pick a time when everyone is going to be out of the house, and no one will be using the water — when the whole family is about to go out shopping or to a movie, for example.
• Before you leave, read the water meter and write down its setting. Then when you get back home, take another reading. If the numbers have changed, you've probably discovered a leak! Tell your parents what you've found.

Another way to be a leak detective: Check your toilet.
• Get an adult to take the top off the toilet tank in your home. Then put about 12 drops of red or blue food coloring in the tank.
• Wait about 15 minutes. Guard the toilet, so no one uses it while you're waiting. That's important.
• Now look in the toilet. If colored water shows up in the bowl, you've found a leak!

(Answer: C. Enough to take 52 baths . . . one for every week of the year.)

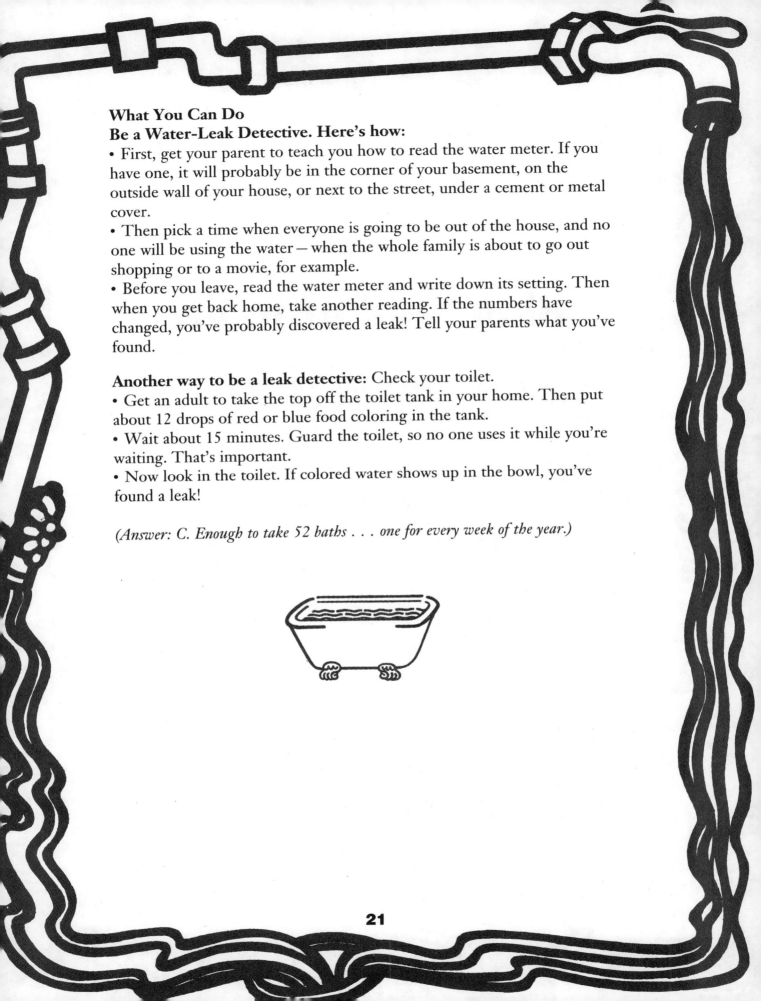

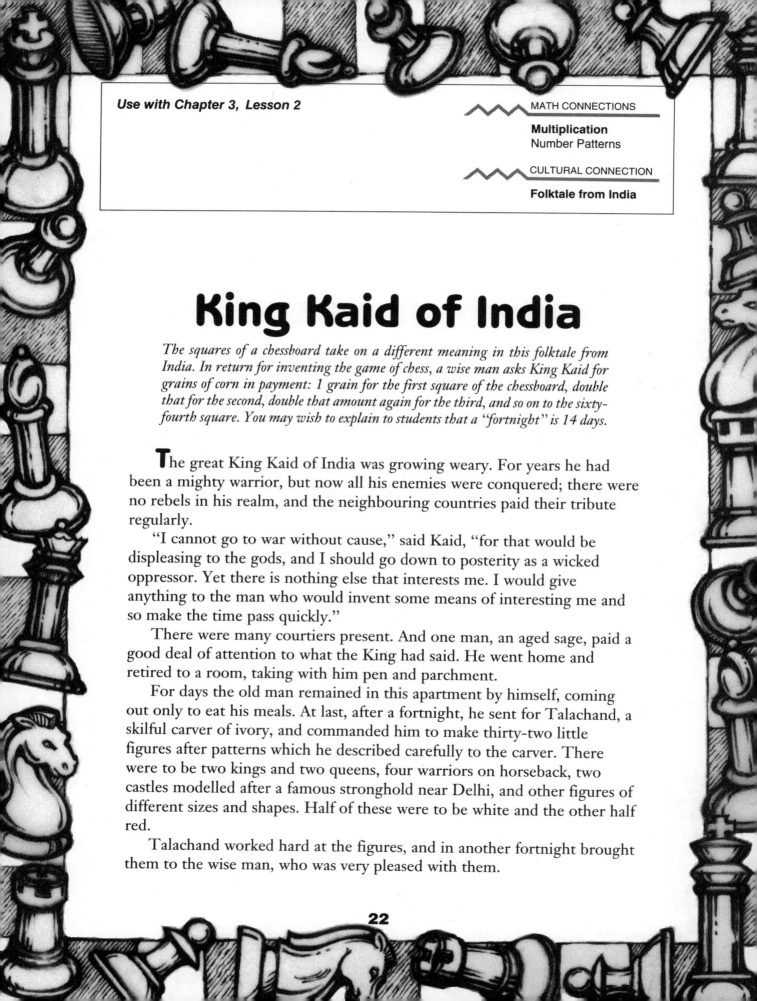

MATH CONNECTIONS

Multiplication
Number Patterns

CULTURAL CONNECTION

Folktale from India

King Kaid of India

The squares of a chessboard take on a different meaning in this folktale from India. In return for inventing the game of chess, a wise man asks King Kaid for grains of corn in payment: 1 grain for the first square of the chessboard, double that for the second, double that amount again for the third, and so on to the sixty-fourth square. You may wish to explain to students that a "fortnight" is 14 days.

The great King Kaid of India was growing weary. For years he had been a mighty warrior, but now all his enemies were conquered; there were no rebels in his realm, and the neighbouring countries paid their tribute regularly.

"I cannot go to war without cause," said Kaid, "for that would be displeasing to the gods, and I should go down to posterity as a wicked oppressor. Yet there is nothing else that interests me. I would give anything to the man who would invent some means of interesting me and so make the time pass quickly."

There were many courtiers present. And one man, an aged sage, paid a good deal of attention to what the King had said. He went home and retired to a room, taking with him pen and parchment.

For days the old man remained in this apartment by himself, coming out only to eat his meals. At last, after a fortnight, he sent for Talachand, a skilful carver of ivory, and commanded him to make thirty-two little figures after patterns which he described carefully to the carver. There were to be two kings and two queens, four warriors on horseback, two castles modelled after a famous stronghold near Delhi, and other figures of different sizes and shapes. Half of these were to be white and the other half red.

Talachand worked hard at the figures, and in another fortnight brought them to the wise man, who was very pleased with them.

Meanwhile, the sage had ordered a curious board from a woodworker in the bazaar. It was square, and contained sixty-four smaller squares, alternately red and white. Such a curious board had not been seen before, and many people were puzzled to think what its use could be.

At last, when the board was finished, and the figures were all ready, the wise man carried them to the King's palace. As soon as his presence was announced, the King summoned him to his chamber.

"Sire," said the old man, "you promised to fulfil any request that might be made by the man who was able to interest your Majesty in some new occupation. Does that promise still hold good?"

"It does," replied the King. "I will do anything for the man who can save me from weariness."

"Well," continued the old man, arranging the ivory figures carefully upon the board in two pairs of rows facing each other, "here is a new kind of warfare for your Majesty, a warfare in which no blood will be shed, no towns burned, no children orphaned, but which will give you plenty of excitement and tax all your powers of strategy if you are to win."

Already the King was interested; and, as the old man showed how the warfare of the ivory figures was waged on the battle-ground of the chequered board, the King grew excited and his weariness fled.

"This white king is your Majesty," said the old man; "and, if you are to win the battle, you must keep a clear mind, for it is by skill and not by force that success comes in this war."

Then the old man showed how the different figures were to move on the board, some going across in either direction, and others moving diagonally, while the figures of warriors on horseback moved a little across and then diagonally. Some moved over many squares at one time and others over one square only.

For weeks and weeks the King studied this new kind of warfare, in which no one was slain, and after a time he felt he had made himself a master of it, and he called the game "the King," or "Chess," which means the same thing.

Then the wise man asked for his reward.

"What shall I give you?" questioned the monarch. "Ask me anything you like, and you shall receive it, to the half of my kingdom."

"I want neither gold nor jewels," said the old man. "All I ask is that your Majesty shall give me one grain of corn for the first square on the chessboard double that for the second square, double that again for the third, and so on — that is, I am to have one, two, four, eight, sixteen, and so on up to the sixty-fourth square; simply that, and nothing more."

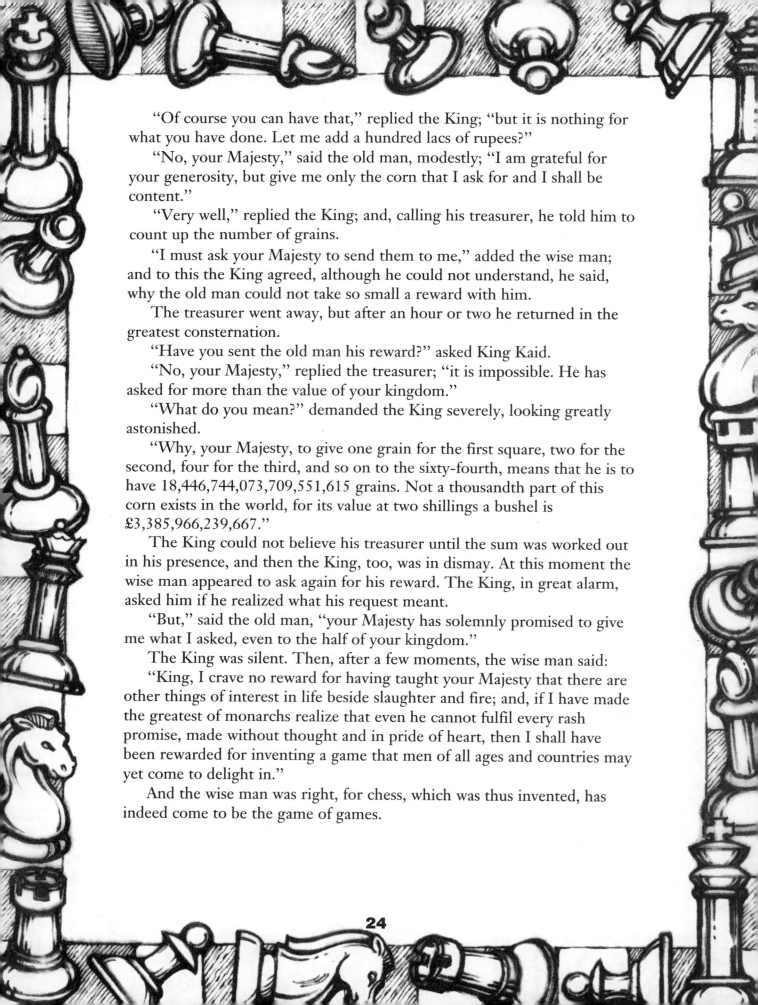

"Of course you can have that," replied the King; "but it is nothing for what you have done. Let me add a hundred lacs of rupees?"

"No, your Majesty," said the old man, modestly; "I am grateful for your generosity, but give me only the corn that I ask for and I shall be content."

"Very well," replied the King; and, calling his treasurer, he told him to count up the number of grains.

"I must ask your Majesty to send them to me," added the wise man; and to this the King agreed, although he could not understand, he said, why the old man could not take so small a reward with him.

The treasurer went away, but after an hour or two he returned in the greatest consternation.

"Have you sent the old man his reward?" asked King Kaid.

"No, your Majesty," replied the treasurer; "it is impossible. He has asked for more than the value of your kingdom."

"What do you mean?" demanded the King severely, looking greatly astonished.

"Why, your Majesty, to give one grain for the first square, two for the second, four for the third, and so on to the sixty-fourth, means that he is to have 18,446,744,073,709,551,615 grains. Not a thousandth part of this corn exists in the world, for its value at two shillings a bushel is £3,385,966,239,667."

The King could not believe his treasurer until the sum was worked out in his presence, and then the King, too, was in dismay. At this moment the wise man appeared to ask again for his reward. The King, in great alarm, asked him if he realized what his request meant.

"But," said the old man, "your Majesty has solemnly promised to give me what I asked, even to the half of your kingdom."

The King was silent. Then, after a few moments, the wise man said:

"King, I crave no reward for having taught your Majesty that there are other things of interest in life beside slaughter and fire; and, if I have made the greatest of monarchs realize that even he cannot fulfil every rash promise, made without thought and in pride of heart, then I shall have been rewarded for inventing a game that men of all ages and countries may yet come to delight in."

And the wise man was right, for chess, which was thus invented, has indeed come to be the game of games.

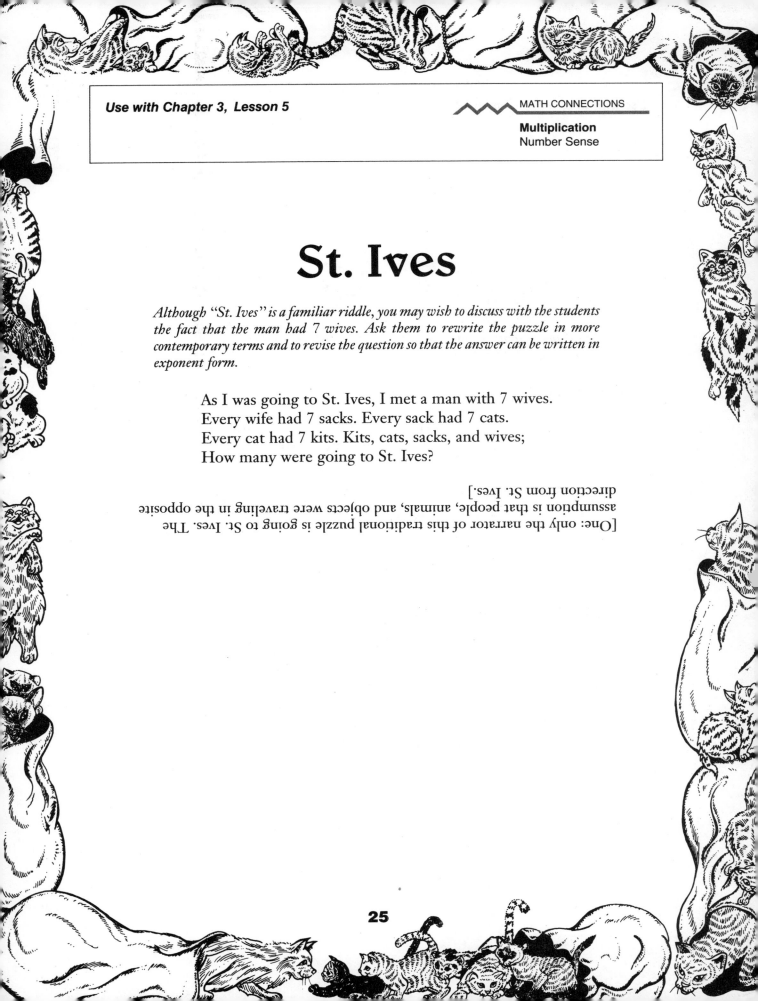

St. Ives

Although "St. Ives" is a familiar riddle, you may wish to discuss with the students the fact that the man had 7 wives. Ask them to rewrite the puzzle in more contemporary terms and to revise the question so that the answer can be written in exponent form.

As I was going to St. Ives, I met a man with 7 wives.
Every wife had 7 sacks. Every sack had 7 cats.
Every cat had 7 kits. Kits, cats, sacks, and wives;
How many were going to St. Ives?

[One: only the narrator of this traditional puzzle is going to St. Ives. The assumption is that people, animals, and objects were traveling in the opposite direction from St. Ives.]

Week Before A Monday Meet:

Specifying beginning times for each day's workout will give students an opportunity to study elapsed time.

Sunday And Wednesday.   Exercises.

Jog 4 minutes. Run 6 minutes at 1/2 speed.
Walk 2 minutes. Repeat 2 times.
         Run 3 minutes at 3/4 speed.
Walk 2 minutes. Repeat 3 times.
         Run 60 seconds: hard.
Walk 60 seconds. Repeat 2 times.
         Run 5-10 minutes.
         Sprint at end.
Jog 6 minutes to cool down.

Monday And Thursday.   Exercises.
Jog 4 minutes: easy.
Run 10 minutes: nonstop. Walk 3 minutes.
Run 60 seconds at 3/4 speed.
         Walk 60 seconds.
         Repeat 4 times.
Run 5 minutes as hard as you can.
Jog 6 minutes to cool down.

Tuesday And Friday.   Exercises. Jog 5 minutes: easy.
Run 4 minutes at 3/4 speed.
Jog 4 minutes: nonstop. Repeat 3 times.
Run 45 seconds. Walk 60 seconds.
Repeat 4 times.
Run 8 minutes: nonstop. Sprint at end.
Jog 6 minutes to cool down.

Saturday.   Warm up.   Exercises.   Run 20 minutes: nonstop.

Sunday. R e l a x. E a t i c e c r e a m.

BY ARNOLD ADOFF

MATH CONNECTIONS

Problem Solving
Addition
Subtraction
Multiplication
Division

Father and Son

FROM Puzzles, Patterns, and Pastimes
BY CHARLES F. LINN

Students will enjoy utilizing the guess, check, and revise strategy to find the ages of the father and son. Can they construct their own puzzles about their own ages and that of a family member or friend?

My father's age I just found out.
He's four times as old as me,
But after only five more years
His age'll be mine times three.

You can sure guess what I'll ask of you,
So speak without delay.
My father's age — and also mine —
Quick now, what do you say?

(Pa is forty and I'm ten . . . but gaining on him.)

28

Use with Chapter 6, Lesson 12

MATH CONNECTIONS

Measurement
Geometry
Fractions
Estimation

Mystery Yarn

An Excerpt From *Homer Price*
BY ROBERT MCCLOSKEY

*In discussing this selection with students, emphasize that the story was published in
1943 and point out how perceptions about women's and men's roles have changed.
To find out how Miss Terwilliger won the contest, tell students to pay attention to
the color of her dress.*

*In addition to measurement, the balls of string can be used as the basis for activities
in geometry, fractions, and estimation.*

. . . **Y**es, Uncle Telly was a string saver and he had saved string for
years and years. He had quite a lot of it too. And every Thursday afternoon
he would take all of the pieces of string that he had collected during the
week and wind them on his huge ball out in the garage. That was one of
Homer's jobs on Thursdays, helping Uncle Telly wind string, because
Uncle Telly had had a bit of rheumatism of late. You see, the ball of string
was getting too large to wind without a lot of stooping and reaching.

Uncle Telly greeted Homer at the door, "Hello, Homer, we've got a
lot to wind today!"

"That's good, Uncle Telly, I brought a few pieces from home too!"

They went out to the garage and as Uncle Telly looked at his ball of
string he said with pride, "Another quarter inch and it'll be six feet
across . . . biggest ball of string in the world."

"Well, I don't know, Uncle Telly," said Homer, "Freddy's been
helping the sheriff wind his string down at the jail, and he says the sheriff's
ball of string is just about six feet across too."

"Humph! I've heard tell that the sheriff winds his string loose, so's the
ball looks bigger. Mine's wound *tight*," said Uncle Telly poking the ball,
"and it's a lot longer than the sheriff's ball of string'll ever be."

29

"Yep!" I guess you're right," said Homer, and he began winding the string while Uncle Telly tied the pieces together in double knots.

"Wind it tight," reminded Uncle Telly, "don't let anybody say that my string isn't wound right! I'll have none of this loose, sloppy, sheriff kind of winding on my ball o'string!"

Just as Homer and Uncle Telly were about finished there was a knock on the garage door and when Uncle Telly opened the door there stood the sheriff and Judge Shank.

"Good day, Telemachus!" said the judge.

"Howdy, Telly," said the sheriff, trying to peer over Uncle Telly's shoulder and see the ball of string.

"Howdy, Judge," said Uncle Telly, and scowling at the sheriff he said, "I didn't expect *you'd* be calling on *me* on a Thursday afternoon."

"Ahem, Telemachus," said the judge, "I just happened to stop in the knitting shop to drive my wife home when I met the sheriff. As you know Telly, — er Telemachus, it is necessary to cut down expenses at the fair this year, and we cannot afford to have the trotting races that we have always had. The sheriff, who like myself is on the fair board, and who, like yourself, is a string saver has suggested that he, and you, Telemachus, enter into an event that could be held on the race track, and provide the diversion that the trotting races have . . ."

"Yep!" interrupted the sheriff, "I challenge you to unroll your string around the race track, just to prove once and for all that I've got more string than you have."

"Er, yes, to put it bluntly, that is the situation, Telemachus. I appeal to your sense of county pride. Do not spurn the offer. And then, of course, the winner will receive a prize . . ."

"I'll *do* it, by Zeus!" said Uncle Telly. "We'll see who's got the most string, Sheriff! Your ball might be just as big as mine but it ain't wound tight." And to prove his point Uncle Telly gave his ball a kick and almost lost his balance.

"Very well, gentlemen," said the judge, "I shall . . ."

"Wait a minute, Judge," interrupted Uncle Telly, "I mean, I'll do it on one condition." (Uncle Telly was noted for driving a hard bargain and Homer wondered just what it would be.) "If I win this here contest, the sheriff has to promise to spend his Thursday afternoons out of town and give Miss Terwilliger a chance to make up her mind to marry me."

"Well," said the sheriff, "in that case, if *I* win you'll have to leave town on Sundays, and give Miss Terwilliger a chance to make up her mind to marry *me!*"

"It's a deal," said Uncle Telly, and he and the sheriff shook hands for the first time in years (just to clinch the bargain of course).

"Very well, gentlemen," crooned the judge, "I shall judge this contest, and at our earliest convenience we will draw up a set of rules pertaining . . . Good day, Telemachus."

"G'by Telly," said the sheriff, "sorry I can't stay but I got an appointment."

Uncle Telly slammed the door on the sheriff and went back to tying knots.

"We'll see!" he said, and pulled the next knot so hard that he broke the string.

"Golly, Uncle Telly," said Homer. "That's going to be a swell contest. I hope you win the prize."

"Uhumpf! Prize or no prize we'll see who's got the most," said Uncle Telly, "and Miss Terwilliger will get a chance to make up her mind. That woman certainly can cook!" sighed Uncle Telly with a dreamy look. Then he busied himself with his knots and said, "Now mind you, Homer, wind it tight."

In the Friday night edition of the *Centerburg Bugle* Homer read a long article on the county fair, and a special announcement about the contest to determine the world's champion string saver, and then the rules that Judge Shank had drawn up.

"Each contestant may appoint an assistant to help with the maneuvering of his ball of string."

"The balls of string shall be unwound, i.e., rolled around the county fair race track in a counter clockwise direction, starting from the judge's booth in front of the main grandstand."

"The ball of string reaching around the race track the greatest number of times shall be regarded as the winning string, and that string's owner shall be declared winner of the prize and of the title of World's Champion String Saver. The string shall be unwound for two hours every afternoon of the week of the fair, starting at two o'clock."

Homer read the rules and noticed that nothing was mentioned about the gentlemen's agreement between the sheriff and Uncle Telly, but that sort of news travels fast in a town the size of Centerburg, and it wasn't long before practically everybody knew that the winner was *supposed* to have the hand of Miss Terwilliger in marriage.

Homer decided to go past Uncle Telly's house and see what he thought about the rules.

Homer couldn't help wondering what a woman who could cook fried chicken so well, and who was as *clever* as Miss Terwilliger would do if *she* heard about the agreement.

Homer found Uncle Telly trying to figure out how many miles of string were wound on his ball. He was multiplying 3.1416 by the diameter and after multiplying by several figures he asked Homer how many feet in a mile.

"Five thousand, two hundred and eighty," said Homer.

Then Uncle Telly multiplied by four. Then he turned to Homer and said, "I figure there's enough string to go around that race track a hundred times. Yep! Twenty-five miles of string! Just let the sheriff beat that if he can!"

"Look, Uncle Telly, here comes the judge and the sheriff again, and look who's with them, *Miss Terwilliger!*"

Uncle Telly opened the door before the judge had a chance to knock, and the judge puffed in, followed by the sheriff and Miss Terwilliger.

"Ah, phuf! Ha, good day, Ha, Phuf! Telemachus, Haah! We have a new contestant for the title of World's Champion String Saver!" puffed the judge.

Miss Terwilliger blushed and giggled while Uncle Telly backed around to the other side of the room and raised his eyebrows at the sheriff in a way that asked, "Did *you* tell her about the agreement?" The sheriff shrugged his shoulders and wiggled his mustache that showed he was just as puzzled as Uncle Telly.

Miss Terwilliger (if she did know about the agreement) wasn't admitting it. "Isn't it *wonderful*," she said to Uncle Telemachus and the sheriff, "that we have *so* much in common?"

"Yes," she tittered, "I've been a savin' string for the past fifteen years! All of the colored yarn and odds and ends from knitting classes. I have a beautiful ball of yarn, all colors of the rainbow."

"Splendid!" said the judge, rubbing his hands together. "Simply splendid, Miss Terwilliger!"

"But Judge," interrupted Uncle Telly anxiously.

"Do you think," said the sheriff, nudging the judge, and winking frantically, "that a *woman* should enter into a sing of this thort, I mean, thing of this sort?"

"Splendid!" continued the judge, ignoring these interruptions. "The American female is beginning to find her rightful place in the business and public life of this nation. The sheriff and Telemachus and I deeply appreciate your public spirit, Miss Terwilliger, and I'm sure that the country fair will be an unprecedented success."

"Come, Judge," said Miss Terwilliger with a smile, "I must get back to my knitting shop. Good-by Sheriff, good-by Telemachus, I'll see *you* on Sunday."

After the judge and Miss Terwilliger were gone the sheriff and Uncle Telly each accused the other of telling about the agreement. They finally calmed down and decided that the judge had double crossed them with his fancy speech about "woman's rights."

"But Uncle Telly," said Homer, "there couldn't be *three* balls of string in the world as large as yours and the sheriff's."

"You're wrong, son!" said the sheriff with a sigh. "Her ball of string's *bigger* than mine! She's a clever woman, son, a *very* clever woman."

"If she wins," said Uncle Telly gloomily, "we'll be right back where we started from, waiting forever for her to make up her mind."

During the next week the whole county got excited about the contest to determine the world's champion string saver. Everybody started saving string for their favorite contestant. The ladies in Miss Terwilliger's knitting classes reported that Miss Terwilliger was knitting a brand new dress for the occasion. When Homer's mother heard this she called Aunt Aggy and said, "We should do something about Uncle Telly. You know how men are about clothes. They can hardly tell one dress or suit from another." The next day they dragged Uncle Telly down town and picked out a nice new and very becoming plaid suit for him. The sheriff said, "If they're going to make a shashion fow, I mean fashion show, out of this thing I can dress up, too!" He sent away special delivery to Chicago and ordered an expertly fashioned double-breasted Hollywood model suit. On the day before the fair started, Homer went up to Miss Terwilliger's with the sheriff to see them take her ball of string out of the house. Mr. Olson, the carpenter, had to take out the side of the house because the ball just wouldn't go through the door. When the moving men rolled it out and on to the truck, the sheriff said, "That's as purty a ball a string as I've ever seen. It's got a toman's woutch! I mean a woman's touch!"

Just then Uncle Telly walked up and agreed, "It's awful pretty, being all colors of the rainbow, but it ain't wound tight. It's so soft you can poke your fist into it."

"Yes, but yarn stretches purty much," said the sheriff unhappily.

The day the fair opened the grandstand was crowded and people stood half-way around the track when the contestants and their assistants started unrolling their string. Miss Terwilliger's new pink dress and the sheriff's and Uncle Telly's new suits caused much favorable comment from the ladies present. The men were more interested in the string, but as Homer's mother said, "They can hardly tell one dress or suit from another." Miss Terwilliger and the sheriff and Uncle Telly were hot and tired after the first two times around the track and so were their assistants. So the judge had some of the regular country fair employees roll the balls while the contestants rode around the track alongside in the sheriff's car.

After the first afternoon's unrolling, Miss Terwilliger's ball measured 5'9"; the sheriff's measured 5'8¾"; Uncle Telly's 5'8". Uncle Telly and the sheriff were very uneasy. At the end of the second day the sheriff's and Miss Terwilliger's 5'; Uncle Telly's 4' 11$\frac{15}{16}$". Uncle Telly felt a little better, and so did the sheriff.

The measurements at the end of the next to the last day of the fair were Uncle Telly and the sheriff running 16½", and Miss Terwilliger only 12⅝", and each contestant's ball of string had unrolled around the track ninety-nine times.

Uncle Telly and the sheriff were feeling pretty confident now, and each one was sure of winning the title of world's champion string saver *and* the hand of the clever Miss Terwilliger.

On the last day of the contest everybody in Center County was on hand early. The contestants were going to roll their balls of string around the track themselves. The sheriff and Uncle Telly were all dressed up for the occasion but Miss Terwilliger was not wearing her new knit dress. The ladies noticed right away that she was wearing the old robin's-egg-blue one that she had saved all these years. She started off carrying her ball in a gay little basket and a parasol to protect her from the autumn sun. She marched right off at 2:00 with her string trailing behind her.

Most everybody knew that Miss Terwilliger's ball was 3⅜" less across than the sheriff's or Uncle Telly's and they admired her confidence and her spirit, but they all knew that she couldn't win.

Uncle T. and the sheriff, each feeling confident, were taking it slow. They watched each other like hawks, and they unwound their string right up against the fence and checked up on each other's knots. They hadn't even gotten a quarter of the way around when Miss Terwilliger was at the half-way mark.

Homer could see her walking right along wearing her robin's-egg-blue dress with the pink trim at the bottom, carrying her basket and the parasol to protect her from the autumn sun. The sheriff and Telly were half-way around still checking every knot and stretching their string as tight as they dared against the fence.

Now Miss Terwilliger was three-quarters of the way around, still walking right along wearing her robin's-egg-blue blouse with the pink skirt, carrying her basket and the parasol to protect her from the autumn sun.

Uncle Telly shouted at the three-quarters mark, "I've won! The sheriff wound his string around a walnut! Mine's solid to the core!"

Everybody started shouting "Hurrah for Telly! Hurrah for Telly the world's champion string saver!" And after the noise had died down people heard another shout, "I've won!" And then they noticed for the first time that Miss Terwilliger was standing right down in front of the grandstand wearing her dress with the robin's-egg-blue trim at the neck and sleeves, holding her basket and the parasol to protect her from the autumn sun.

The judge puffed down to where Miss Terwilliger was and held up the end of her string and shouted, "I pronounce you the winner of the title of String Saving Champion of the World!"

Then everybody started cheering for Miss Terwilliger.

Uncle Ulysses and the sheriff trudged up and congratulated Miss Terwilliger, and told her how glad they were that she had won the championship. Everyone could see though that they were unhappy about having to wait forever for her to make up her mind—especially Uncle Telly.

Practically every woman who was there that day knew how the clever Miss Terwilliger had won the championship. They enjoyed it immensely and laughed among themselves, but they didn't give away the secret because they thought, "all's fair in love," and besides a woman ought to be allowed to make up her own mind.

There *might* have been a few *very* observing men, who like Homer, knew how she won. But they didn't say anything either, or, maybe they just didn't get around to mentioning it before Miss Terwilliger finally decided to marry Uncle Telly the following week. It was a grand wedding with the sheriff as best man.

Uncle Telemachus and his new wife left for Niagara Falls, while the guests at the reception were still drinking punch and eating wedding cake, and doughnuts—not to mention fried chicken.

"That was a wandy dedding, I mean a dandy wedding!" said the sheriff to Homer while polishing off a chicken breast. He looked at the wishbone and sighed. Then after a minute he brightened and said, "But they've asked me to dinner every Thursday night!"

"You know, Homer," said the sheriff with a smile, "they'll be a very cappy houple, I mean, happy couple, going through life savin' string together."

"Yep," said Homer, "I guess they're the undisputed champions now."

"Guess you're right, Homer, nobody'll *ever* get so much string saved on one ball as they have . . . Heck, I think I'll start savin' paper bags or bottle caps!"

Archimedes and the King's Gold Crown

BY LINDA WALVOORD GIRARD

Archimedes wrestled with the problem of trying to determine if the king's crown was made of solid gold. The sight of water flowing out of his tub helped Archimedes find the solution. This story may also be used to introduce metric units of measure in Chapter 5.

King Hiero, who lived in Syracuse on the island of Sicily, had a new crown of solid gold. The king had given his goldsmith pure gold and ordered him to hammer and mold it into just the crown the king wanted.

At last the crown was finished, and the king wore it all day. It was rather large, but the king was happy, for kings love to wear golden crowns that sway a bit as they walk.

Not until King Hiero was ready to go to sleep did he reach up to remove the crown. Hmm, he said to himself. This solid gold crown isn't as heavy as I thought it would be. It looks like solid gold. It shines. It's the right size. But it seems a bit light. He bounced it in his hands.

A black thought crept into the king's mind. Maybe his royal goldsmith had cheated him by melting the gold and mixing it with silver. Silver is much lighter than gold, and it's also cheaper than gold. Every king knows that. Had the goldsmith kept some of that gold for himself, and had he stretched out the gold for the king's crown with silver?

All night the king lay awake worrying about his crown. By morning he knew what to do. "Wrap up my crown and get a horse ready," King Hiero said to his courier. "You must take my crown to Archimedes. I have a great problem and I need a smart man like him to solve it."

When Archimedes received the king's courier, he was astonished.

There lay the crown, sparkling in the sunlight, and with it the king's secret message about his suspicions.

Archimedes was flattered by the king's trust. But he was worried, too, for he had no idea how he could answer the king. How could he *prove* beyond all doubt that the crown was or was not pure gold? He couldn't just lift the crown himself and say to the king, "Yes, it's the right weight, I think." Or, "No, it's too light, I think." He needed a scientific way to test that crown.

In his fine laboratory Archimedes put the king's crown on one side of a scale, and pieces of pure, shining gold on the other until they balanced. He had the crown's weight in gold. But now what? Now, whenever Archimedes was puzzled by a problem, he did two things to make his great brain work even harder. First, he talked to himself, repeating the facts. What did he know? Well, he knew the crown had been made to the exact size the king had ordered. He knew its weight in gold. And he knew that gold is more dense than silver. Or that, for the same volume (the amount of space), gold is heavier than silver.

The second thing Archimedes always did — his secret trick in solving problems — was to form a lot of "If, then — " sentences.

He started imagining crowns in his mind. If two crowns, one gold and one silver, were the same size, he thought, then the gold crown would be heavier. And if two crowns, one gold and one silver, were the same weight, then the silver crown would be larger. If two crowns were both solid gold and were exactly the same size, then they must also weigh the same. And, he thought, putting his hand on his forehead and closing his eyes, if two crowns were both pure gold, and both weighed the same, then . . . then they would also be the same size.

But now what?

Something was missing — a way to compare the size. He wished he could squash the crown somehow, like a mass of clay, into one hunk, without all the turrets and curves, so he could see its real size. Or else, he wished he could take those gold hunks himself and fashion them into a copy of the crown, the exact size of the king's.

But I can't do that, Archimedes thought. I am not a goldsmith. I am a philosopher, a thinker, a mathematician. I have to think my way out of this.

But he was stumped.

At last, hours later, Archimedes was ready to give up and go home for dinner. He was hot. So he decided he would stop at the baths.

At the bath chamber a servant filled the tub to the rim. Archimedes was tired. He sighed as he stepped in. *Whoosh. Splash.* As he sank into the tub with an *aah*, water flowed over the rim. And that's when something clicked in his mind. The water that spilled out was making room for whatever went into the tub. When he sank into that tub, his body was taking up space. The amount of water that had spilled was exactly the same amount of space that he had occupied.

Well, that was it. The spilled water was a way to measure size!

Archimedes was so happy that he leaped out of the tub and ran naked out of the bathhouse into the streets, laughing, shouting, and crying, *"Eureka!"* which is Greek for "I have found it!"

The passers-by all stared. "Oh well, it's only Archimedes the philosopher," one man said. "He's a little crazy. Somebody get him a towel."

It wasn't long before Archimedes stood in the king's royal court, watching the goldsmith swagger in and sit down.

"What's this all about? I'm busy," the goldsmith said.

"Archimedes, please proceed," said the king.

Archimedes now brought forth his scale and his gold weights, his water, his bowls, and the king's crown.

"What are you doing, preparing lunch?" asked the goldsmith.

Archimedes put the crown on one side of his scale. Then he put gold weights on the other side of the scale, just as he had done in his laboratory. "I have here," said Archimedes, pointing to the perfectly balanced scale, "the exact weight of this lovely crown in pure gold."

Archimedes then asked a servant to fill two bowls exactly to the rim with water and to be ready to catch the water that overflowed.

Archimedes took the pure gold weights from the scale and lowered them into a large bowl of water. The servants caught all the water that spilled out as the gold sank.

Next, Archimedes lowered the crown into the second water-filled bowl. Again, the servant caught all the water that spilled out as the crown sank.

"I now have two amounts of water," Archimedes announced.

"Congratulations," said the goldsmith with a brave sneer. "So what?"

But the king knew so what. Archimedes held up the two glass containers of water that had spilled.

The king stood up. "So they are not the same," he said, glaring at the goldsmith. "If my crown were gold through and through, then it would spill exactly the same amount of water as its weight in gold. But it didn't; it spilled more. So you cheated me. You used something else!"

Within five minutes the king had clapped the greedy goldsmith into prison. And that very day he ordered the crown melted down and made over of pure gold. And the king gave many honors and gifts to Archimedes for solving his problem.

Today the name of that king is hardly remembered. His kingdom is gone. And the crown is lost.

But because Archimedes saw something in a new way and used it to solve a problem, his name has never been forgotten. Today we'd call him a true scientist. You might remember him, too, whenever you lean back in your bath and — *whoosh*, *slosh* — the water moves to make room for you.

Use with Chapter 7, Lesson 7

MATH CONNECTIONS

Fractions
Addition
Subtraction
Multiplication
Division

Mathemagician

BY SANDRA LIATSOS

This poem can spark discussion not only about fractions but also about students'
perceptions of mathematics.

I think I'll practice being
a marvelous mathemagician
knowing instant answers
to any tough addition.
My mind like a computer
will quickly multiply
birds, monkeys, or bananas
quick as a winking eye.

No number will defeat me,
not even the smallest fraction.
One/one millionth of a bug
will spark my math to action.

Subtracting candies from a jar
will by my greatest pleasure.
And when we find old, pirate gold
I'll divide our treasure
Without a minute's worry
over answers right or wrong.
With practice all of math will be
like singing a favorite song.

Use with Chapter 7, Lesson 8

MATH CONNECTIONS

Fractions
Multiplication
Division
Measurement

The Lunar Olympics

FROM Einstein Anderson Lights Up the Sky
BY SEYMOUR SIMON

Einstein Anderson and his friend Margaret decide to make a moon scale in the Lunar Olympics at school.

"**H**ow about having a scale that shows what you would weigh on the moon?" Einstein suggested to Margaret. "We can use the balance scale from the school nurse's room. Then we can write the moon weight figures on cardboard and tape them to the scale."

"That's a good idea," replied Margaret. "We'll just divide each of the weight numbers on the scale by six. That will give us the weights on the moon."

"Right," said Einstein. "The moon's gravitational pull is only one-sixth as strong as Earth's. So a person would weigh only one-sixth as much on the moon as on Earth."

"That's a great way to lose weight," said Margaret. "The only trouble is that your mass remains the same, so that you look the same as you do on Earth."

"Let's review what we have so far for the Lunar Olympics. We have a weight lifting contest, and we'll label the weights with numbers one-sixth of their Earth weight—"

"Won't Pat be happy when he can lift a few hundred pounds over his head!" interrupted Margaret.

"Pat is already so bigheaded he can't find an aspirin that will fit him," Einstein agreed. "He's always trying to push himself forward by patting himself on the back."

"Don't get started telling jokes," said Margaret. "We have to stage the Lunar Olympics of the year 2100 at Moon Base I for our class next week.

That means we have to complete the plans today so we know what materials we'll need."

"The materials better not cost too much," said Einstein. "After all, the moon itself is only worth a dollar."

"What?" Margaret asked bewilderedly.

"The moon has four quarters, so it's only worth . . ."

"Never mind, Einstein! Just get on with the plans."

"Sorry about that. Let me see. Besides the weight lifting, we have a shot put contest. Instead of a heavy iron ball, we'll use a baseball painted gray and labeled with a weight six times as heavy as it really is."

"We can have two contests with the ball," said Margaret, "a distance throw and a height throw. Then we can compare the results with a real shot put contest on Earth."

"Say, if an athlete gets athlete's foot, do you know what an astronaut gets?" Einstein asked.

"I'm sure you'll tell me," said Margaret.

"An astronaut gets mistletoe. Get it? Missile-toe."

"I got it," said Margaret, "but I hope it's not catching."

"I wish you'd stop joking around," Einstein laughed. "You're making me into a moon insect—a lunatic. A *lunar tick*. Why aren't you laughing, Margaret?"

"Just get on with it, Einstein," Margaret said, trying to keep from smiling. "Suppose we have a walking race over a hundred-yard course. Only we'll really make the course sixteen yards long. Then we can have a high jump bar labeled six times higher than it really is."

"That's not what would happen on the real moon, Margaret," said Einstein.

"Are you still joking?" asked Margaret. "If you can throw a weight six times as high and six times as far on the moon as you can on Earth, then you should be able to walk six times as fast and jump six times as high as you can on Earth."

"This is no joke," said Einstein. "Although it seems logical, it really isn't."

Can you solve the puzzle: Why can't you walk six times faster and jump six times higher on the moon?

"You'll have to explain that," said Margaret.

"Right," said Einstein. "You see, when you walk on Earth, your body is raised up about one-and-a-half inches with each step. But on the moon it will drop back more slowly than it does on Earth. On the moon you would be walking more slowly than you could walk on earth."

"I think I understand," Margaret said slowly. "But surely a high jumper could jump over a bar six times higher on the moon."

"He could jump over a higher bar, but not six times higher," said Einstein. "The reason has to do with the way he lifts his feet and where his center of gravity is. Let's say that a high jumper is six feet tall. His center of gravity, the point where all his weight is concentrated, is about three-and-a-half feet off the ground. To jump over a six-foot bar, he has to raise his center of gravity only two-and-a-half feet. To clear the bar, he lifts his legs as far up as possible. That means that he really raised his center of gravity only two-and-a-half feet to jump over the six-foot bar. So on the moon he wouldn't be able to jump over a thirty-six-foot-high bar."

"How high could he jump?" asked Margaret.

"He could jump six times the two-and-a-half feet, about fifteen feet high. Then if he raised his legs upward the same as on Earth, he could clear another three-and-a-half feet."

"That means he should be able to jump over a bar about eighteen-and-a-half feet high," Margaret calculated. "That's still a pretty good jump."

"Oh, that's not so good," said Einstein. "I bet you I could jump across the room."

"Let's see you do it," said Margaret.

Einstein walked to the other side of the room and then jumped. "I told you I could jump across the room," he said.

MATH CONNECTIONS

Fractions
Multiplication
Problem Solving

CULTURAL CONNECTION

Folktale from Persia

Molla Nasreddin and His Donkey

A Persian Folk Tale
FROM Eurasian Folk and Fairy Tales
BY I. F. BULATKIN

Without the intercession of Molla Nasreddin and his donkey, the 3 farmers might still be trying to divide 17 donkeys equally among themselves! This selection is the basis for the opener to this chapter.

Three peasants came to market one day to buy donkeys. They found a trader who had seventeen to sell and after they had haggled and bargained until everybody was confused they put their money together and bought the lot. But once they had the donkeys they did not know how to divide them. They puzzled and argued and fought, and finally decided to take the case to a judge.

The judge listened carefully to what they had to say until he learned that, for the seventeen donkeys, the first peasant had paid half the price the trader asked, the second had paid one-third, and the last one-ninth.

The judge thought for a long time and tried his best to solve the problem, but no matter how hard he calculated, he could not find the necessary solution so he could deliver a judgment. Finally he had to give up, and he sent for Molla Nasreddin to come and help him.

Nasreddin mounted his donkey and hurried off to assist the judge. He listened attentively to the complaint of the squabbling peasants and then asked them:

"Well, how do you want to divide the donkeys?"

The peasants answered: "Each of us wants to have as many donkeys as he paid for, and we want them all to be safe and sound and healthy."

Molla stood up and said to them: "Let's go and see the donkeys."

So everybody including the jury went out into the courtyard where the seventeen donkeys were standing. Molla went off and got his own donkey and added him to the lot.

"Now," he said, "there are eighteen."

"Oh, no, Molla," the peasants said, "we don't need your donkey. There's no reason why you should suffer a loss. Just divide ours so that each of us has those he paid for."

"Molla Nasreddin is not so stupid," answered Molla, laughing. "Be patient a little. You will have your donkeys, but mine will remain with me. The great Allah will see to that. Now let us begin." Then he said to the first peasant:

"You told me that you had paid half of the money the trader asked?"

"Yes," was the reply.

Nasreddin counted off nine donkeys from the eighteen.

"Here is your part."

Then he asked the second peasant:

"And you paid one-third, is that true?"

"Yes."

"Therefore you have a right to six. Is that correct?"

"Well, yes. Perhaps a little more."

Finally Molla addressed the third peasant:

"You paid one-ninth of the price, and that comes to two from the eighteen. Isn't that right?"

"That is absolutely right," replied the third man.

Molla Nasreddin gave him two donkeys, and then mounted his own and rode off.

And the judge stood pondering a long, long time about the wisdom of Molla Nasreddin . . . .

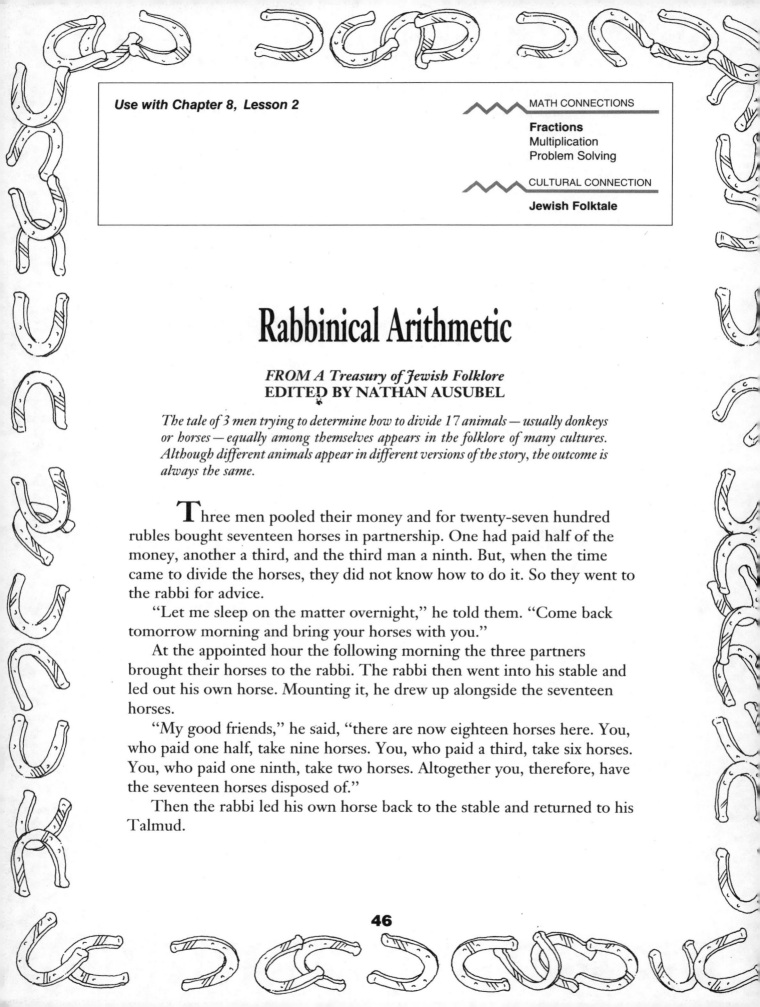

MATH CONNECTIONS

Fractions
Multiplication
Problem Solving

CULTURAL CONNECTION

Jewish Folktale

Rabbinical Arithmetic

FROM A Treasury of Jewish Folklore
EDITED BY NATHAN AUSUBEL

The tale of 3 men trying to determine how to divide 17 animals — usually donkeys or horses — equally among themselves appears in the folklore of many cultures. Although different animals appear in different versions of the story, the outcome is always the same.

Three men pooled their money and for twenty-seven hundred rubles bought seventeen horses in partnership. One had paid half of the money, another a third, and the third man a ninth. But, when the time came to divide the horses, they did not know how to do it. So they went to the rabbi for advice.

"Let me sleep on the matter overnight," he told them. "Come back tomorrow morning and bring your horses with you."

At the appointed hour the following morning the three partners brought their horses to the rabbi. The rabbi then went into his stable and led out his own horse. Mounting it, he drew up alongside the seventeen horses.

"My good friends," he said, "there are now eighteen horses here. You, who paid one half, take nine horses. You, who paid a third, take six horses. You, who paid one ninth, take two horses. Altogether you, therefore, have the seventeen horses disposed of."

Then the rabbi led his own horse back to the stable and returned to his Talmud.

Life in Flatland

ADAPTED FROM *FLATLAND*
BY A. SQUARE

We live in a world of three dimensions — length, height, and width. What would it be like if the world had only two dimensions? The book Flatland *was written nearly one hundred years ago. The author, A. Square (his real name was Edwin Abbott) had a unique viewpoint. In his imaginary world, all the people are Triangles, Squares, Circles, and other flat shapes.*

I call our world Flatland — not because this is what we call it, but so that you will know what it is like. You must understand at once that in my country there is nothing of the kind you call a solid shape. As you know, a solid, or three-dimensional shape, has length, width, and thickness. But in Flatland, everything is flat. That is, there are only two dimensions — length and width.

Imagine a huge sheet of paper on which Straight Lines, Triangles, Squares, Pentagons, Hexagons, and other shapes move freely about, very much like shadows. You will then have a pretty correct idea of what my country and countrymen look like. You might think that we can tell Triangles, Squares, and other flat shapes by sight. But this is not so. We cannot tell one shape from another. We can see only Straight Lines. Let me show you why this is so.

Place a penny in the middle of a table. Now, lean over the table and look straight down upon the penny. It will appear to be a Circle.

But, move back to the edge of the table and lower your head. When your eyes are exactly level with the edge of the table (so that you are, as it were, a Flatlander) the penny will no longer look like a Circle. It will seem to have become, so far as you can see, a Straight Line.

The very same thing will happen if you take a piece of cardboard and cut out a Triangle, or Square, or any other shape. Put the shape on a table and look at it from the edge of the table. You will find that you see only a Straight Line.

Well, that is exactly what we see in Flatland when we meet a friend. As our friend comes ever closer to us, the line becomes larger and brighter. When our friend goes away from us, the line becomes smaller and dimmer. Our friend may be a Triangle, Square, Pentagon, Hexagon, or any other shape, but all we see is a Straight Line.

You may wonder how we can tell one friend from another. I will explain in a moment. But first, let me now tell you about the kinds of people there are in Flatland.

Our Soldiers are Straight Lines. I shall have more to say about them shortly.

All our Farmers are Isosceles Triangles, with two equal sides, each about eleven inches (27 centimeters) long. The third side is quite short, often not much more than half an inch (12 millimeters). This causes the two equal sides to form a very sharp angle that is most useful for plowing.

Our Merchants and Shopkeepers, of whom there are many, are Equilateral, or Equal-Sided, Triangles.

Most of our fine Doctors and Lawyers are Squares, like myself. But a few, who have risen to the top of their profession, are Five-Sided shapes, or Pentagons.

There are several degress of School Teachers, beginning with Six-Sided shapes, or Hexagons, and going on to shapes that have many more sides. Finally, we have our Philosophers, who are the wisest of all our people. They have so many sides, and the sides are so small, that they cannot be distinguished from a Circle.

There are many dangers in Flatland, just as there are in your world. The greatest of these dangers is our shapes. We have to be careful not to bump into one another. A Flatlander who has a sharp shape can easily hurt another person. For this reason, our sharply pointed Farmer Triangles are quite dangerous.

This being so, you can see that our Soldiers are far more dangerous. If a Farmer is like an arrowhead, a Soldier is like a needle, inasmuch as a Soldier is all point (for a line, as you know, is made up entirely of points). Add to this the power Soldiers have of making themselves almost invisible and you can easily see that a Soldier of Flatland is not a person to trifle with!

Perhaps you are wondering how our Soldiers can make themselves invisible. Let me explain.

Place a needle on a table. Then, with your eye at the edge of the table, look at the needle sideways. You will see the whole length of it. But look at it end-ways and you see nothing but a point. It has become practically invisible. This is how it is with all of our Soldiers. When a Soldier's side is turned toward us, we see a Straight Line. When the end containing the Soldier's eye faces us, we see nothing but a rather gleaming point. But when a Soldier's back is to us, it is a dim point that is almost impossible to see.

You can understand, then, how dangerous our Soldiers are. You can get a gash by running into a Merchant Triangle. And you can be quite badly wounded in a collision with a Farmer Triangle. But it is nothing less than absolute death to bump into a Soldier! And when a Soldier is seen only as a dim point, it is difficult, even for the most cautious, to avoid a collision!

For this reason, our Soldiers must be careful. When any Soldiers are out in the street, either standing or walking about, they must move their backs constantly from side to side so that anyone behind them will be able to see them.

You lucky people who live in a world of three dimensions are blessed with shade as well as light. You enjoy many colors. You can see an angle and the complete shape of a Circle. But in Flatland, we do not have these blessings. How, then, can I make you understand the difficulty we have recognizing one another?

The first means of recognition is the sense of hearing. Our hearing is keener and more highly developed than is yours. It enables us not only to tell the voices of our friends, but even to tell the difference between shapes, at least for the Triangle, the Square, and the Pentagon.

But feeling is the best way of recognizing another Flatlander. What an "introduction" is to you, feeling is with us. However, you must not think that feeling is as slow and difficult for us as it might be for you. Long practice and training, which begins in school and goes on throughout life, make it possible for us to quickly tell the difference between the angles of an Equal-Sided Triangle, a Square, or a Pentagon.

It is not necessary, as a rule, to do more than feel a single angle to tell a person's shape, unless he or she belongs to the higher class of shapes. That makes it much more difficult. Even the professors in our University of Wentbridge have been known to confuse a Ten-Sided Polygon with a Twelve-Sided one. And there is hardly a Doctor of Science anywhere in Flatland who would know at once, just by feeling a single angle, the difference between a Twenty-Sided and a Twenty-Four-Sided shape.

Many of us prefer still a third method, which is recognition by the sense of sight.

That this power exists anywhere, and for any class, is the result of Fog. For Fog is present everywhere during most of the year, except in the very hot parts of Flatland. For you, fog is a bad thing that hides the landscape,

makes you feel poorly, and damages your health. But for us, Fog is a blessing, nearly as important as the air itself!

If there were no Fog, all our friends would look like exactly the same kind of Straight Line. But wherever there is a rich supply of Fog, an object only slightly farther away than another is a bit dimmer than the nearer object. So, by carefully examining the dimness and brightness of things, we are able to tell the exact shape of an object.

For example, suppose I were to see two people coming toward me. Let us say that one is a Merchant (an Equilateral Triangle) and the other is a Doctor (a Pentagon). Both appear to be Straight Lines, so how am I to tell one from the other?

In the case of the Merchant, I see a Straight Line, of course. The center of this line, which is the part nearest to me, is very bright. But on either side, the line fades away rapidly into the Fog. I can tell at once, then, that the line slants back quite sharply from the center.

On the other hand, the Doctor has a slightly different appearance. As with the Merchant, I see only a Straight Line with a very bright center. On either side, the Doctor's line also fades into the Fog, but not as rapidly as the Merchant's line. Thus I can tell at once that the Doctor's line does not slant back as sharply. Because of the slight difference in brightness, I know that one shape is an Equilateral Triangle and that the other is a Pentagon.

But enough about how we recognize one another. Let me now say a word or two about our climate and our houses.

Just as you do, we have four points of the compass: North, South, East, and West. But because there is no sun — or, indeed, any other heavenly body — in Flatland, it is impossible for us to tell North in the way you do. However, we have a method of our own.

By a Law of Nature in Flatland, there is a constant pull from the South. This pull is quite enough to serve as a compass in most parts of Flatland. Moreover, the rain, which falls at regular times each day, comes always from the North, so this is an additional help. And in the towns we have the help of the houses, for every house is built with the roof pointing North, to keep off the rain.

However, in our more northern regions, the pull of the South is hardly felt. Sometimes, when walking across an open plain where there have been no houses to guide me, I have had to stand and wait for hours until the rain came. Only then could I be sure of the direction in which I was going.

Our houses are quite comfortable and very well suited to our climate and way of life. The most common form of house construction in Flatland is Five-Sided, or Pentagon-Shaped.

The two northern sides make up the roof, and usually have no doors. On the east, there is the door by which we go in. On the west side, there is another door by which we go out. In this way, we are able to go in and out without bumping into and hurting one another. The south side, or floor, is usually doorless.

Square and Triangular houses are not allowed. There is a good reason for this. The angles of a Square (and still more of a Triangle) are much more pointed than the angles of a Pentagon. The lines of houses and almost all other objects are dimmer than the lines of Men and Women. Therefore, there is a danger that the points of a Square or Triangular house might do serious injury to an absent-minded traveler suddenly running against them.

As early as the eleventh-century of our era, Triangular houses were forbidden by law. The only exceptions were forts and similar kinds of buildings, where the sharp points might serve a useful purpose. At this period, Square houses were still permitted. But about three centuries later, the Law decided (for reasons of public safety) that in all towns with a population above ten thousand, the angle of the Pentagon was the smallest house angle that could be allowed. It is only now and then, in some very remote and backward farming district, that one may still discover a Square house.

We have no windows in our houses. This is because light comes to us both inside and outside, by day and by night, equally at all times and in all places. But where light comes from, we do not know. In the old days, our wise men liked to try to discover the cause of light, but this filled our hospitals with those who went mad trying to solve the problem.

I — alas, I alone in Flatland — know the true solution to this mysterious problem. But I cannot make my knowledge understandable to a single one of my countrymen. I am mocked at — I, the only one who knows the truth: that light comes from your strange world of three dimensions!

My Knee Is Only Sprained

FROM Sports Pages
BY ARNOLD ADOFF

What would our bodies look like if our knees or elbows or heads could swivel 360 degrees? If our ankles turned completely around, would our feet go in opposite directions? Making angles by bending their elbows and knees will enhance students' understanding of measuring angles.

My Knee Is   Only   Sprained,

         is   only   swollen,
and
the   doctor   says   I   will   be
            fine.
      I'll   play   again.

      He   says   this   as   he
      sits   on   his   padded
      leather   chair   that
      can   swivel   360 de
         grees.
      Oh
        why   can't   knees?

Still.   We   do   not   make   the   Six   O'Clock   News
        with   this   old   story,   often   told,   of
           pain   and   frustration   and   fear.
Still.
        I   must   sit   on   this   bench   and   be   as
still   as   this   brace   demands;
    as
still   as   the   other   spectators   behind   me   in
              the   stands.
I   have   been   told: next   season,
        next   y e ar.

The Roads of Math

BY JEFFREY DIELLE

The roads of math begin with a straight line and then become a triangle, a cone, a circle (with diameter and circumference — let's not forget pi), a square, and back to a straight line again!

Take a straight line,
 And divide it into three.
Make the three lines form three angles,
 And a triangle have we.

Now take this little triangle
 And twirl it about in space.
Twirl the triangle 'round and 'round;
 A cone is what we face.

Now look at the bottom of our cone.
 We see a circle true.
Now let's examine the circle
 And what it can do for you.

Let's draw a line through the center
 Of our circle round.
We've discovered something new:
 The diameter we've found.

53

Let's look at the line 'round the circle.
    The circumference says, "Hi!"
Divide the circumference by the diameter,
    And we've found the number Pi.

Now take our semicircle
    And take a point on the rim.
Using the diameter form a triangle.
    (It doesn't take much vim.)

Look carefully at this triangle.
    If you do, something different you'll see,
For the largest of its angles
    Has exactly ninety degrees.

Now take two of these new right angles.
    Put their vertices in the circle's
        center, there.
With the diameter under one side of
        each angle,
We're ready to form a square.

Mark the points on the circumference
    Where the right angles do fall.
Construct triangles in both semicircles,
    And that is all.

From a line, to a triangle, to a cone,
    To a circle, to Pi, to a square.
We have traveled the roads of math,
    Which will take you anywhere.

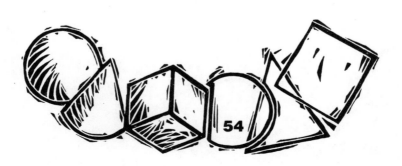

The World in His Hands

FROM Einstein Anderson Lights Up the Sky
BY SEYMOUR SIMON

Einstein Anderson's friend Stanley wants to build a scale model of the solar system in his basement. But as Einstein points out, there's only one problem — the size of Stanley's basement.

Stanley Roberts was a good friend of Einstein Anderson's, even though he was older and a junior at Sparta Senior High School. Stanley was very much interested in science and often invited Einstein to come over and see his inventions and experiments.

"This time I've really got something big in mind," Stanley said, pushing aside some flasks and test tubes on his laboratory table. "Let me show you my plans."

Stanley's "laboratory" was really the attic room that his mom and dad had permitted him to use for his experiments. It was in its usual messy state. Bunsen burners, glassware, aquariums, small animal cages, and half-finished models were everywhere. It looked like a junk shop, but Stanley claimed it was all scientific apparatus.

"Something really big," asked Einstein, "like the giant ants or the green monster that you were going to send for through the mail?"

"Those were just silly mistakes," Stanley said, brushing back his black hair, which kept falling into his eyes. "This is different. It's really scientific. And you can help me construct it and share in the profits."

"Help you? How?" Einstein asked cautiously. "You're not still thinking of making an exercise machine, I hope. It worked fine when I used it. But when you sat down in that machine, the gears jammed. By the time I got it fixed and you got out, your muscles were so sore you couldn't play baseball for a week."

"No, no," said Stanley impatiently. "This is something completely different. You've been to a planetarium, haven't you?"

"Isn't that an all-star show?" Einstein asked him innocently.

"Well, you know how crowded the planetarium gets," Stanley said, ignoring Einstein's joke. "Can you imagine how much money we can make when I open a planetarium in my basement and charge admission?"

"Are you kidding?" said Einstein. "Do you know how difficult and expensive it is to construct a planetarium? Why, the star projector alone can cost thousands of dollars."

"This won't be that kind of planetarium," Stanley admitted. "It will really be just the solar system in the middle of the basement with star photos around the walls. The main attraction will be the sun and the planets."

"That reminds me of a joke, Stanley. Do you know what the little planet said when it went out of its orbit?"

"Huh?" said Stanley.

"Look, Ma, no gravities!"

Stanley groaned. "Forget those terrible jokes," he said. "Look at this advertisement I'm going to answer and tell me if this isn't the best idea I've ever had."

"Right," said Einstein, looking at the magazine Stanley handed him. "I see you're still using authoritative scientific journals for your science ideas. *Thrilling Science Fiction Stories* is a great magazine for finding real science advertisements."

"Just read the ad," Stanley said warningly.

"O.K.," Einstein said hastily. He read the advertisement slowly. Then he looked up at Stanley. "This is an advertisement for scale models of Earth, the other planets of the solar system, and the sun."

"That's right. Isn't it a great idea? They'll send me an eight-inch-diameter model of Earth along with detailed plans for the sun and all the other planets to scale. I'll build the models exactly and then place them in my basement, using the same scale for their distances from the sun. Then I'll use large photos of the stars for the walls. It'll be spectacular!"

"Let me get this straight," said Einstein. "You plan to build a scale model of the solar system, put it in your basement, and charge admission to see it?"

"You've got it," Stanley said happily.

"I've got it," said Einstein, "but I don't think you have. Your idea is interesting. But it will never work."

Can you solve the puzzle: What's wrong with Stanley's plans to build a model of the solar system in his basement?

"I don't see why not," Stanley said. "It shouldn't be too difficult to make models of the sun and the other planets. We can use clay or something like that for the models."

"You'll need an awful lot of clay," said Einstein. "Let's say that Earth is represented by an eight-inch globe. Earth is about eight thousand miles in diameter, so on that scale one inch equals one thousand miles. Jupiter, the largest planet in the solar system, is more than eighty-eight thousand miles in diameter. A model of Jupiter built to the same scale as the model of Earth would have to be eighty-eight inches in diameter, more than seven feet across."

"Oh, oh," said Stanley. "I forgot to check into the sizes of the planets."

"It's not even the planets you'd have most to worry about," said Einstein. "It's the sun. The sun's diameter is more than eight hundred and sixty thousand miles. That means a scale model of the sun would be eight hundred and sixty inches across, more than seventy-one feet."

"I'll never get that into my basement," Stanley said, "but maybe we can find a hall that's big enough."

"Forget it," said Einstein. "Even if you did find a hall big enough for the models, it would still be too small to place them away from the sun in the same scale. Earth is ninety-three million miles from the sun. It would have to be ninety-three thousand inches away from the sun, or more than one mile away."

"I told you I had a big idea," Stanley said sadly.

"You have no idea how big," Einstein said. "Earth is one of the planets that's closest to the sun. But the most distant planet on average is Pluto. It's three thousand six hundred and seventy million miles from the sun. On the same scale as the model of Earth you would have to place Pluto nearly seven hundred *miles* away!"

"Wow!" exclaimed Stanley. "How wrong can I be!"

"Cheer up," said Einstein. "Nothing is all wrong. Even a broken clock is right twice a day."

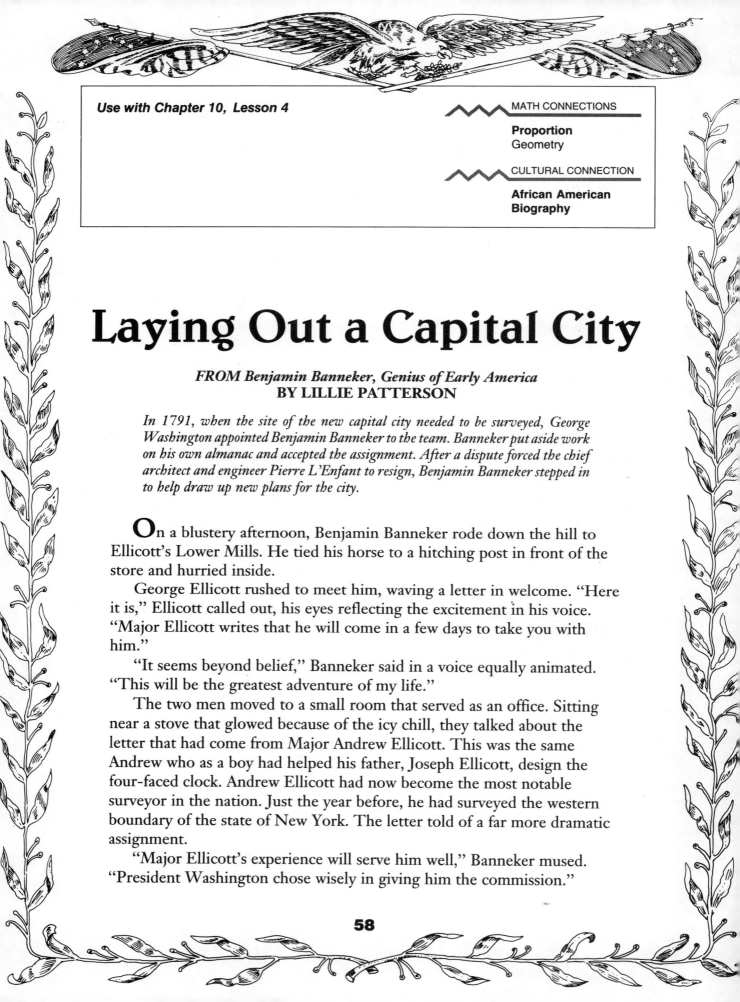

MATH CONNECTIONS

Proportion
Geometry

CULTURAL CONNECTION

**African American
Biography**

Laying Out a Capital City

FROM Benjamin Banneker, Genius of Early America
BY LILLIE PATTERSON

In 1791, when the site of the new capital city needed to be surveyed, George Washington appointed Benjamin Banneker to the team. Banneker put aside work on his own almanac and accepted the assignment. After a dispute forced the chief architect and engineer Pierre L'Enfant to resign, Benjamin Banneker stepped in to help draw up new plans for the city.

On a blustery afternoon, Benjamin Banneker rode down the hill to Ellicott's Lower Mills. He tied his horse to a hitching post in front of the store and hurried inside.

George Ellicott rushed to meet him, waving a letter in welcome. "Here it is," Ellicott called out, his eyes reflecting the excitement in his voice. "Major Ellicott writes that he will come in a few days to take you with him."

"It seems beyond belief," Banneker said in a voice equally animated. "This will be the greatest adventure of my life."

The two men moved to a small room that served as an office. Sitting near a stove that glowed because of the icy chill, they talked about the letter that had come from Major Andrew Ellicott. This was the same Andrew who as a boy had helped his father, Joseph Ellicott, design the four-faced clock. Andrew Ellicott had now become the most notable surveyor in the nation. Just the year before, he had surveyed the western boundary of the state of New York. The letter told of a far more dramatic assignment.

"Major Ellicott's experience will serve him well," Banneker mused. "President Washington chose wisely in giving him the commission."

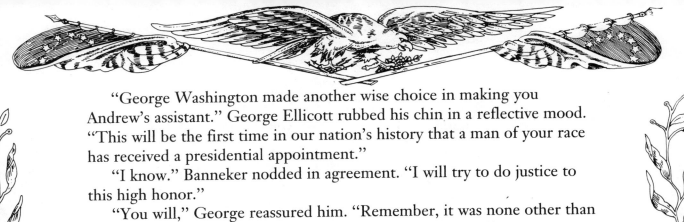

"George Washington made another wise choice in making you Andrew's assistant." George Ellicott rubbed his chin in a reflective mood. "This will be the first time in our nation's history that a man of your race has received a presidential appointment."

"I know." Banneker nodded in agreement. "I will try to do justice to this high honor."

"You will," George reassured him. "Remember, it was none other than Thomas Jefferson who urged the President to appoint you."

The voices of Banneker and George Ellicott quickened as they talked over the events that had led to the receipt of the letter. The surveying task was part of a new undertaking by the young United States. Until this time the Congress had temporarily been sitting in first one city, then another — eight cities in all. Now Congress decided that the nation should have a permanent capital city.

But where? Congress left the choice to the President. In 1790 George Washington selected a centrally located spot near the majestic Potomac River, between the states of Maryland and Virginia. Each state donated a parcel of land for the project.

This ten-mile-square federal district had to be surveyed before the city could be built. In January, 1791, President Washington decreed that this survey should be made, and Andrew Ellicott was the logical choice.

Ellicott, in turn, needed an assistant with skills in both astronomy and mathematics. The President and Thomas Jefferson, who was then secretary of state, readily agreed that Benjamin Banneker should be appointed for this position.

The recalling of these events that February day ended with Banneker and George Ellicott shaking hands gravely. They knew that the task ahead was a difficult challenge. The results could affect the development and the destiny of the country. A dynamic capital city, Americans hoped, would unite the various sections of the country, resulting in a strong union.

Suddenly, a look of consternation crossed Banneker's face. "My almanac! I must complete calculations for my almanac."

"Your country comes first," George Ellicott said firmly. "Besides, I know that nothing is going to keep you from taking on this challenge."

So it was that Benjamin Banneker rode home and began preparing for his new adventure. Minta and Molly shared his pride in the assignment. Their oldest sister was now dead, but her son, John Henden, kept in touch with Banneker. John Henden promised to keep an eye on the place while his uncle was away. Molly's son, Greenbury Morton, agreed to care for the animals and the orchard.

What should he take with him? Banneker pondered this problem as he

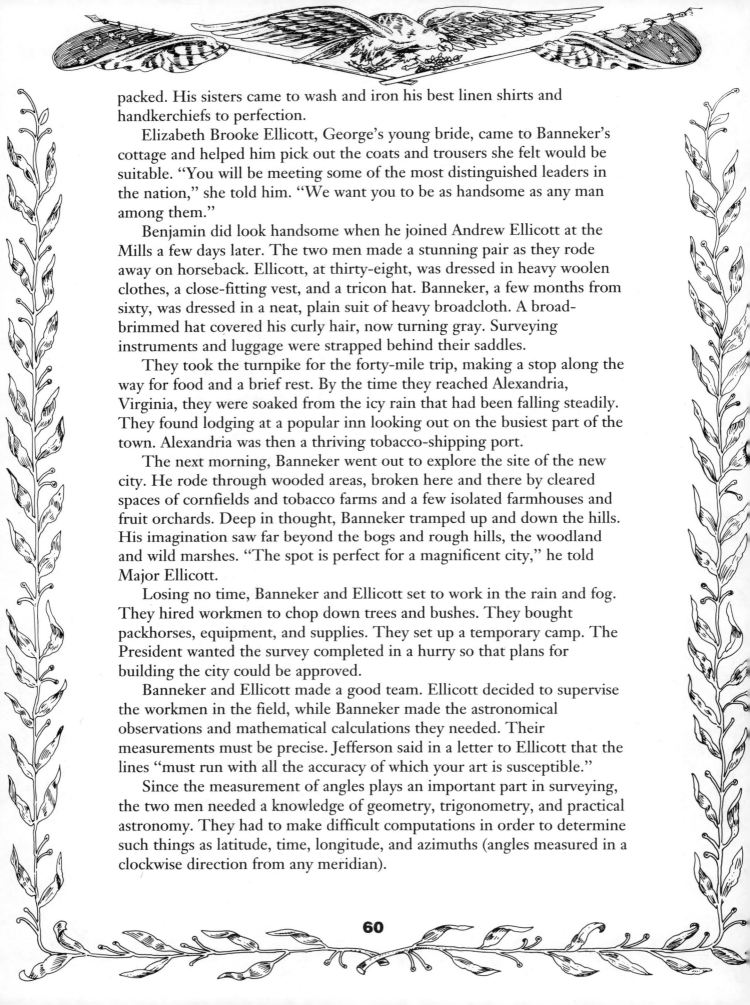

packed. His sisters came to wash and iron his best linen shirts and handkerchiefs to perfection.

Elizabeth Brooke Ellicott, George's young bride, came to Banneker's cottage and helped him pick out the coats and trousers she felt would be suitable. "You will be meeting some of the most distinguished leaders in the nation," she told him. "We want you to be as handsome as any man among them."

Benjamin did look handsome when he joined Andrew Ellicott at the Mills a few days later. The two men made a stunning pair as they rode away on horseback. Ellicott, at thirty-eight, was dressed in heavy woolen clothes, a close-fitting vest, and a tricon hat. Banneker, a few months from sixty, was dressed in a neat, plain suit of heavy broadcloth. A broad-brimmed hat covered his curly hair, now turning gray. Surveying instruments and luggage were strapped behind their saddles.

They took the turnpike for the forty-mile trip, making a stop along the way for food and a brief rest. By the time they reached Alexandria, Virginia, they were soaked from the icy rain that had been falling steadily. They found lodging at a popular inn looking out on the busiest part of the town. Alexandria was then a thriving tobacco-shipping port.

The next morning, Banneker went out to explore the site of the new city. He rode through wooded areas, broken here and there by cleared spaces of cornfields and tobacco farms and a few isolated farmhouses and fruit orchards. Deep in thought, Banneker tramped up and down the hills. His imagination saw far beyond the bogs and rough hills, the woodland and wild marshes. "The spot is perfect for a magnificent city," he told Major Ellicott.

Losing no time, Banneker and Ellicott set to work in the rain and fog. They hired workmen to chop down trees and bushes. They bought packhorses, equipment, and supplies. They set up a temporary camp. The President wanted the survey completed in a hurry so that plans for building the city could be approved.

Banneker and Ellicott made a good team. Ellicott decided to supervise the workmen in the field, while Banneker made the astronomical observations and mathematical calculations they needed. Their measurements must be precise. Jefferson said in a letter to Ellicott that the lines "must run with all the accuracy of which your art is susceptible."

Since the measurement of angles plays an important part in surveying, the two men needed a knowledge of geometry, trigonometry, and practical astronomy. They had to make difficult computations in order to determine such things as latitude, time, longitude, and azimuths (angles measured in a clockwise direction from any meridian).

And these computations were based upon observations made of the sun, stars, and other celestial objects. In making these observations, the heavenly bodies are assumed to be situated on the surface of a huge imaginary "celestial sphere" whose center is at the center of the earth. So, the measurement of horizontal and vertical angles could be done in relation to celestial objects.

This required an observatory tent. Ellicott and Banneker placed the tent upon the highest point of a hill. A hole was left open at the top, through which the sky could be observed. Major Ellicott owned some of the finest surveying and astronomical instruments in the world, along with some of the most up-to-date reference books. Banneker made up his mind to master both instruments and books. The observatory tent became his world. He even slept there.

By the end of the first week, the weather cleared enough for Banneker to make his first observations. The powerful telescopic instruments magnified the stars in a manner he had never imagined. After a time, he was expertly recording the position and movement of stars, sun, and planets. To avoid errors, he repeated the charting again and again, then took an average of the results. It was tiring, tedious work, but Banneker loved every minute of it.

In his sky-watching, Banneker became fascinated by astronomical time-telling. Ellicott gave him the responsibility for caring for his precious astronomical clock. There were only a few of them in existence. The precision timepiece, set in a tall case, needed constant attention. Banneker kept it wound and checked it periodically against his observation of the sun so that the time would remain correct. An astronomical clock, in addition to having a dial for local time, has dials to record positions of the moon, stars, and planets, along with a variety of other astronomical data.

Night after night, Banneker worked while others slept. By the time the sun rose over the tent, Major Ellicott would arrive from nearby George Town, where he slept. Sometimes Banneker would go with him to do field surveying, but more often he stayed to work in the tent. In late afternoon he got a chance to sleep, but even then workmen came into the tent to ask questions, or he had to get up to check the clock by the sun. He kept this heavy schedule, seven days a week, with no word of complaint.

By the end of February the surveying was well under way. In March the engineer-architect began his work of designing the city. President Washington appointed Major Pierre Charles L'Enfant for this task. L'Enfant had come to America from his native France as a volunteer to fight with the American colonies during the War for Independence. He adopted the United States as his home and began a career of designing buildings and medals. It was L'Enfant who designed the Order of the

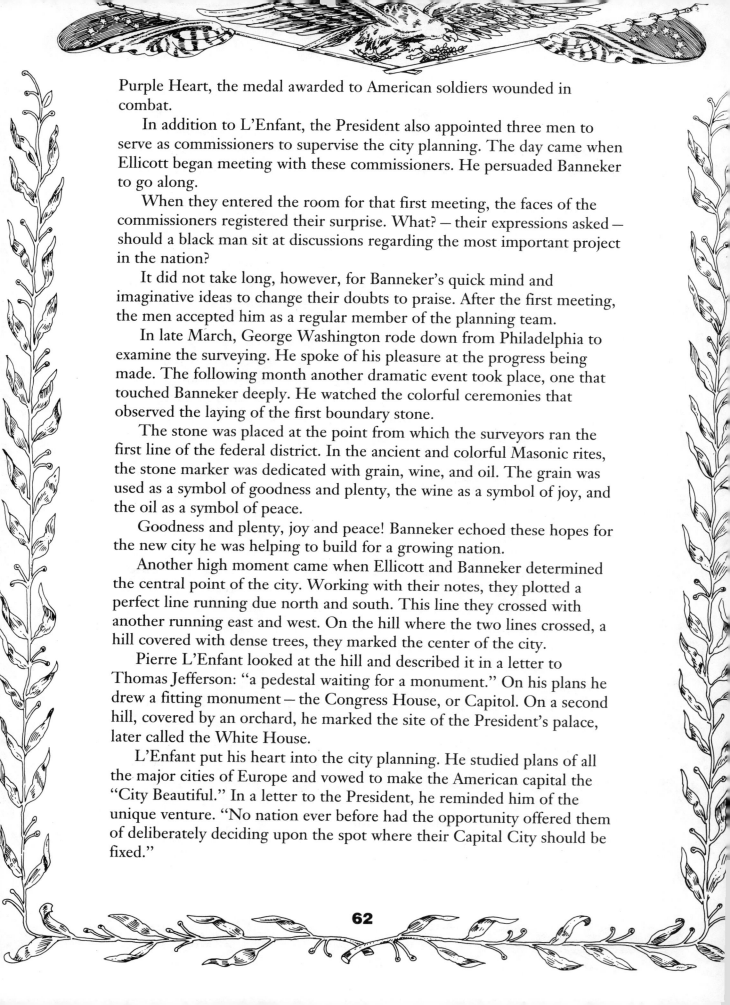

Purple Heart, the medal awarded to American soldiers wounded in combat.

In addition to L'Enfant, the President also appointed three men to serve as commissioners to supervise the city planning. The day came when Ellicott began meeting with these commissioners. He persuaded Banneker to go along.

When they entered the room for that first meeting, the faces of the commissioners registered their surprise. What? — their expressions asked — should a black man sit at discussions regarding the most important project in the nation?

It did not take long, however, for Banneker's quick mind and imaginative ideas to change their doubts to praise. After the first meeting, the men accepted him as a regular member of the planning team.

In late March, George Washington rode down from Philadelphia to examine the surveying. He spoke of his pleasure at the progress being made. The following month another dramatic event took place, one that touched Banneker deeply. He watched the colorful ceremonies that observed the laying of the first boundary stone.

The stone was placed at the point from which the surveyors ran the first line of the federal district. In the ancient and colorful Masonic rites, the stone marker was dedicated with grain, wine, and oil. The grain was used as a symbol of goodness and plenty, the wine as a symbol of joy, and the oil as a symbol of peace.

Goodness and plenty, joy and peace! Banneker echoed these hopes for the new city he was helping to build for a growing nation.

Another high moment came when Ellicott and Banneker determined the central point of the city. Working with their notes, they plotted a perfect line running due north and south. This line they crossed with another running east and west. On the hill where the two lines crossed, a hill covered with dense trees, they marked the center of the city.

Pierre L'Enfant looked at the hill and described it in a letter to Thomas Jefferson: "a pedestal waiting for a monument." On his plans he drew a fitting monument — the Congress House, or Capitol. On a second hill, covered by an orchard, he marked the site of the President's palace, later called the White House.

L'Enfant put his heart into the city planning. He studied plans of all the major cities of Europe and vowed to make the American capital the "City Beautiful." In a letter to the President, he reminded him of the unique venture. "No nation ever before had the opportunity offered them of deliberately deciding upon the spot where their Capital City should be fixed."

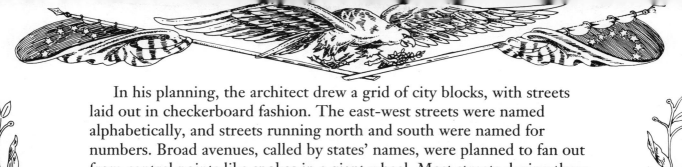

In his planning, the architect drew a grid of city blocks, with streets laid out in checkerboard fashion. The east-west streets were named alphabetically, and streets running north and south were named for numbers. Broad avenues, called by states' names, were planned to fan out from central points like spokes in a giant wheel. Most streets during these times were less than fifty feet across. L'Enfant planned for streets over one hundred feet wide and for one grand avenue four times wider. To add to the symmetrical beauty of the city, the architect planned public parks, fountains, circles, and monuments.

Benjamin Banneker thrilled to the idea of these grand plans. He liked L'Enfant, and whenever he got a chance to talk with him or to learn details of his plans, he made the most of the opportunity.

Unfortunately, the commissioners did not share this admiration. "Good land is being wasted to make wide avenues," they complained. "There are too many public parks."

"Make no little plans when building a capital," L'Enfant said in answer. "The city must be magnificent enough to grace a great nation."

The commissioners demanded maps of the plans so that lots could be sold. L'Enfant refused, knowing that land speculators would buy up choice spots.

The friction came to a crisis when the nephew of one of the commissioners began building a manor house on a spot that would block a major avenue.

"The streets and avenues must be laid out before houses go up helter-skelter," L'Enfant insisted.

The powerful landowner refused to move the structure. So L'Enfant sent a crew of workmen to dismantle the half-finished house and move the materials out of the way.

This was too much for the city commissioners. They complained to President Washington. At that time the President and Jefferson were busy with problems of running the country. The two sided with the commissioners. Reluctantly, the President notified L'Enfant that his services were at an end.

Deeply hurt and heartbroken, L'Enfant left, taking most of his completed plans with him. With his departure, Washington and Jefferson were left with a ten-mile square of muddy land and no plans for changing it into a city. If the project took too long, Congress might well withdraw support and not vote the funds they needed.

The two leaders turned to Andrew Ellicott for help. Could he finish the surveying and map the city as well?

Major Ellicott agreed and turned to his faithful assistant. "Will you help me?" he asked Benjamin Banneker.

"I will assist in every way I can," Banneker readily agreed. By this time he had returned to his home in Maryland and was hard at work on his almanac.

Once again Banneker put aside his own work to help plan the city. Working together, he and Ellicott were able to draw new plans, based upon their knowledge of the designs of Pierre L'Enfant. Their task was not insurmountable because they could use notes from their actual survey of the ground. Fortunately for America, the plans were eventually completed.

In later years, many people have insisted that it was Banneker who saved the city by drawing L'Enfant's plans from memory. Some scholars believe that this story is only part fact and the rest legend.

The bulk of Banneker's notes, which might have given full details, were lost in a tragic fire. Many of Major Ellicott's papers were lost or stolen during another misunderstanding with the commissioners.

What is known beyond the shadow of a doubt is that Banneker assisted in laying out both the federal territory that became the District of Columbia and the capital called Washington City. As he had envisioned, Washington, D.C., developed into one of the most elegant and symmetrical capitals in the world. Visitors from all over the world find pleasure in its spacious, graceful charm. Benjamin Banneker, the self-taught astronomer, helped to create this historic loveliness.

〜〜〜 MATH CONNECTIONS

Percent
Problem Solving
Subtraction

Erin McEwan, Your Days Are Numbered

An Excerpt
BY ALAN RITCHIE

Erin McEwan solves a real-life math problem and earns Mrs. Sbrocchi's gratitude. What's more important, Erin discovers that she's smarter in math than she thought she was.

. . . *A*t six thirty everything was tidied up, and Mrs. Sbrocchi was slumped on a folding chair behind the counter. It was then that Erin admitted she still had an itch to do some more repricing for the sale. Would Mrs. Sbrocchi mind?

"Go ahead, dear," said Mrs. Sbrocchi. "I haven't the heart to face all of that tonight."

So Mrs. Sbrocchi stayed out in front and prepared some food. Erin marched into the back, armed herself with the calculator, and began again to seize cans from the shelf, one at a time, and to calculate the sale price.

Erin had planned to spend only half an hour but soon lost track of the time. Finally she had calculated a price for everything she could find on the storage shelves.

By now she was growing a little tired of calculating twenty percent reductions. She was itching to try her percentage skills on something else. She had pushed a whole rat's nest of invoices toward the back of the desk. Now she pulled some forward and took the first invoice off the pile. The invoice showed both a wholesale price and a retail price suggested by the manufacturer. No good for what she wanted. She dug down into the pile and found a small hand-typed bill from the lady who made different kinds of pâté for Mrs. Sbrocchi. There were only wholesale prices typed on the bill — the prices Mrs. Sbrocchi paid for the pâté.

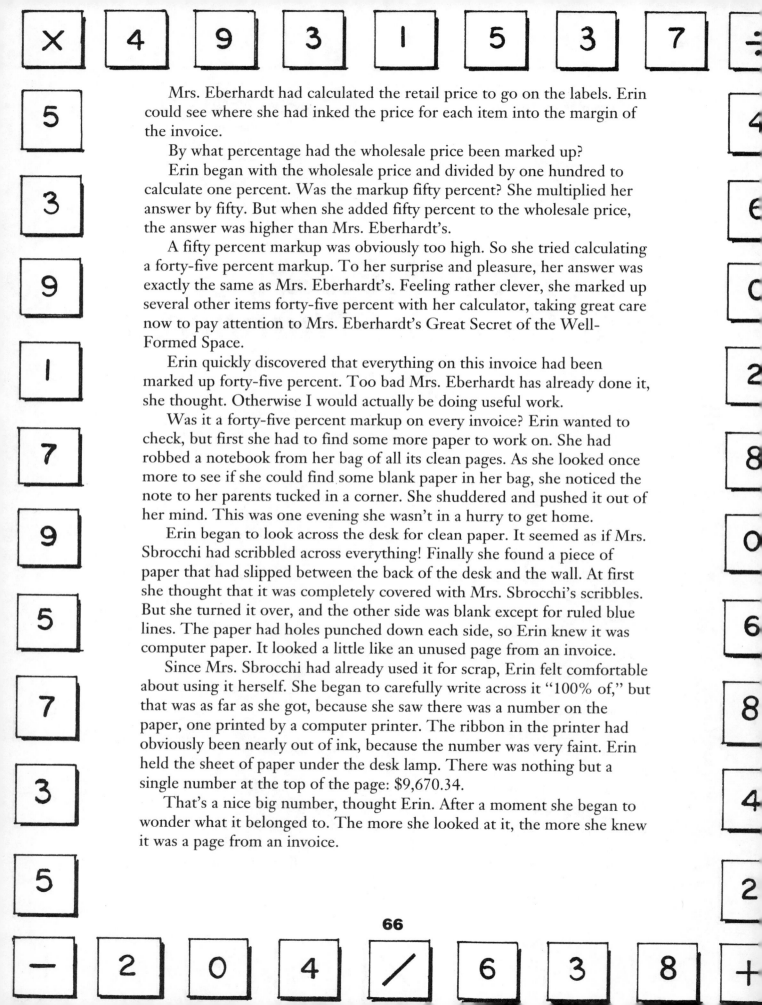

Mrs. Eberhardt had calculated the retail price to go on the labels. Erin could see where she had inked the price for each item into the margin of the invoice.

By what percentage had the wholesale price been marked up?

Erin began with the wholesale price and divided by one hundred to calculate one percent. Was the markup fifty percent? She multiplied her answer by fifty. But when she added fifty percent to the wholesale price, the answer was higher than Mrs. Eberhardt's.

A fifty percent markup was obviously too high. So she tried calculating a forty-five percent markup. To her surprise and pleasure, her answer was exactly the same as Mrs. Eberhardt's. Feeling rather clever, she marked up several other items forty-five percent with her calculator, taking great care now to pay attention to Mrs. Eberhardt's Great Secret of the Well-Formed Space.

Erin quickly discovered that everything on this invoice had been marked up forty-five percent. Too bad Mrs. Eberhardt has already done it, she thought. Otherwise I would actually be doing useful work.

Was it a forty-five percent markup on every invoice? Erin wanted to check, but first she had to find some more paper to work on. She had robbed a notebook from her bag of all its clean pages. As she looked once more to see if she could find some blank paper in her bag, she noticed the note to her parents tucked in a corner. She shuddered and pushed it out of her mind. This was one evening she wasn't in a hurry to get home.

Erin began to look across the desk for clean paper. It seemed as if Mrs. Sbrocchi had scribbled across everything! Finally she found a piece of paper that had slipped between the back of the desk and the wall. At first she thought that it was completely covered with Mrs. Sbrocchi's scribbles. But she turned it over, and the other side was blank except for ruled blue lines. The paper had holes punched down each side, so Erin knew it was computer paper. It looked a little like an unused page from an invoice.

Since Mrs. Sbrocchi had already used it for scrap, Erin felt comfortable about using it herself. She began to carefully write across it "100% of," but that was as far as she got, because she saw there was a number on the paper, one printed by a computer printer. The ribbon in the printer had obviously been nearly out of ink, because the number was very faint. Erin held the sheet of paper under the desk lamp. There was nothing but a single number at the top of the page: $9,670.34.

That's a nice big number, thought Erin. After a moment she began to wonder what it belonged to. The more she looked at it, the more she knew it was a page from an invoice.

After a moment she began to carefully sort through the piles of invoices on the desk. They were all different shapes and sizes. Erin was looking for an invoice with the same color of printing on it, and faint numbers from a bad ribbon.

Not far down in the pile she found what she was looking for. It was an invoice from Wallace Specialty Food Imports, Halifax, Nova Scotia. Erin knew that Wallace Specialty was Mrs. Sbrocchi's largest supplier. Every month a truck arrived and left a large pile of boxes containing all of the many kinds of cans and bottles of strange tidbits that came from European countries.

There was five pages of invoice describing different items and their prices. At the very bottom of the fifth invoice Erin found a line that read, "Subtotal: $8,791.22." There was one more line after that, and it was so faint Erin had to hold it under the light. That line read, "Less 10% on orders over $5,000.00."

There was nothing else on the page. That wasn't surprising—there was no room for anything else. The final total had been pushed off onto a page all of its own—the very page that Mrs. Sbrocchi had turned into scrap paper.

"Less 10% on orders over $5,000.00," Erin read again. Well, this order was definitely more than $5,000.00. This will be fun, she thought, calculating percentages with really big numbers.

So, as she had done before with the invoices, she started off writing carefully, "100% = $8,791.22," then 1% = $8,791.22/100," then "10% = $8,791.22/100 x 10."

Erin calculated the answer and wrote it down: $879.12. Finally she neatly wrote, "$8,791.22 − $879.12 =," and, after using the calculator, penciled in the answer: $7,912.10.

Am I right? she wondered. She looked up at the top of the very sheet she was working on to check the faint number printed there.

It read, "$9,670.34."

Erin frowned. Darn. She had not made a mistake calculating percentages for quite a while now. Oh well, she thought to herself, I guess I'm not perfect after all. She carefully began to write out her calculations all over again with extra care.

Her next answer was exactly the same: $7,912.10. Wrong again. Erin frowned and studied the figures.

Suddenly something became very obvious. I've been taking twenty percent off prices for two days, she thought. The answer is always *less* than I started with, otherwise it wouldn't be a sale, now would it? Ten percent off also had to be less. So why on earth does the invoice say "Less 10%" and then show an answer that is *more*?

The more Erin looked at the problem, the more perplexed she became.

Finally she called in Mrs. Sbrocchi. "I've found something kind of funny," she said, and explained what she had been doing.

Mrs. Sbrocchi was just as puzzled. After a few moments she opened the little safe and took out the company checkbook.

"What was your answer?" said Mrs. Sbrocchi.

"$7,912.10," said Erin, looking at her figures. "Both times I did it."

"That's just what Mrs. Eberhardt wrote on the check," said Mrs. Sbrocchi. Erin was delighted.

"Of course Mrs. Eberhardt didn't have the last page because it was behind the desk," said Mrs. Sbrocchi, thinking hard. "So she must have done the calculation herself."

"But they asked for $9,670.34," said Erin.

"Yes, but she only *gave* them $7,912.10," said Mrs. Sbrocchi. "Which makes a difference of —"

"Wait," commanded Erin, and carefully subtracted.

"$1,758.24," she said.

"In other words, we paid them nearly two thousand dollars less than they asked for," said Mrs. Sbrocchi, who was beginning to get excited. "My accountant started all this by asking why we'd paid out roughly two thousand dollars less than we usually do over the last couple of months." She sat and thought hard for a minute. "I'm beginning to wonder —"

She stood again, opened the filing cabinet that was wedged beside the desk, and began to look through old bills and invoices.

"Here," said Mrs. Sbrocchi, pulling an invoice out of the files and plopping it down in front of Erin. "Last July." She continued to hunt through the files while Erin studied the invoice. The company name at the top was the same, Wallace Specialty Food Imports, but otherwise the invoice looked completely different. It had no holes punched down the sides, and the print on the page was crisp, unlike the little patterns of dots that Erin knew came from computer printers.

Erin turned to the last page of the invoice. The subtotal for the invoice came to a little over six thousand dollars. Below the subtotal was a line that read, "Less 10% on orders over $5,000.00." Erin quickly calculated the ten percent discount.

"This invoice is okay," she announced. "They subtracted the discount like they were supposed to."

"What about this one?" said Mrs. Sbrocchi, putting another invoice in front of Erin. It was dated the previous September and was the same kind of computer invoice as the most recent one.

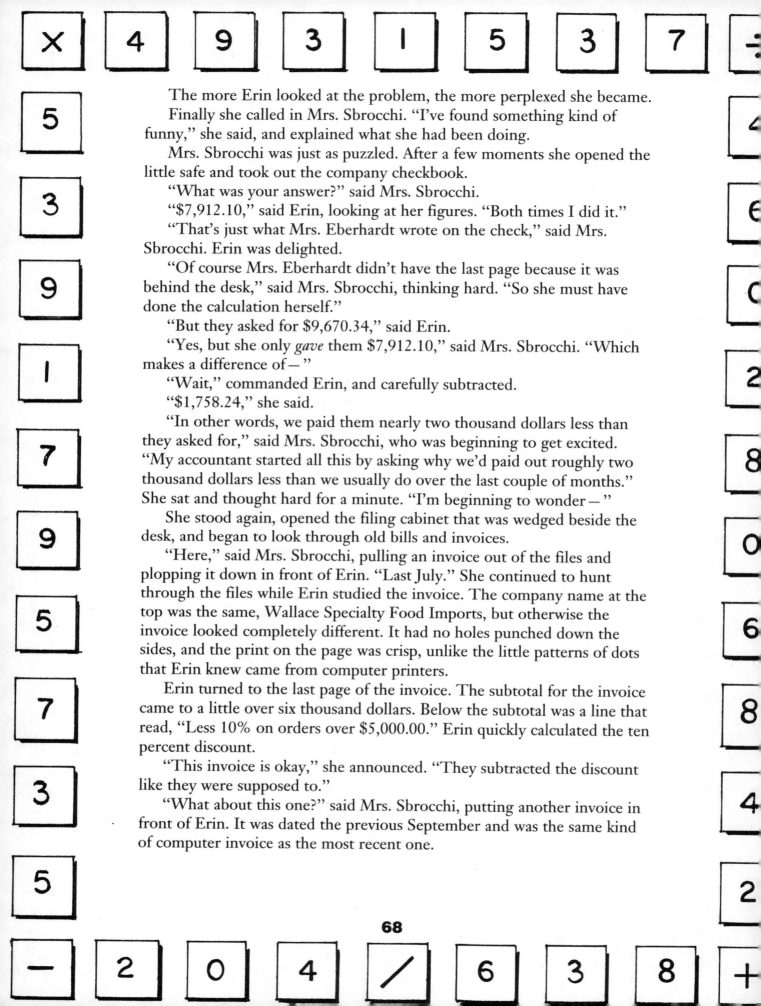

"Nope," said Erin hunched over the calculator. "This one is wrong. They *added* the discount."

"And on this one. It's wrong too," she said a moment later after Mrs. Sbrocchi had handed her a November invoice.

Mrs. Sbrocchi was ecstatic. She had found all the invoices from September to the most recent in May. She quickly looked them over to confirm that Erin's calculations were right.

"Ever since they started computer billing they've been overcharging us!" she said. "Ooo, I could kiss you, Erin!" And she did.

"Not only have you cleared up the mystery of the missing money, it looks like you've earned me about ten thousand dollars that I've been sending to Wallace by mistake!" She picked up one of the invoices and shook her fist at it. "I can't wait to get on the phone with these idiots."

Then she put the invoice down and said more seriously, "Of course, it's partly my fault. I never bothered to check. I just paid what they asked for."

"Oh, Erin!" she said, hugging Erin again. "You've been worth every penny I've paid you, and more. You deserve a bonus for this."

Erin thought she had never been so happy in her life. Just imagine! Solving a math problem! And not just a classroom problem, but a real one. A mystery that had stumped other, older minds. . . .

BLACK ELK SPEAKS

**Being the Life Story of a Holy Man of the Oglala Sioux
as told through JOHN G. NEIHARDT (Flaming Rainbow)**

In his lifetime, Black Elk witnessed the Battle of the Big Horn and the massacre at Wounded Knee. Black Elk expresses his feelings in this section of his biography about the forced move of the Oglala to a reservation.

The First Cure

After the heyoka ceremony, I came to live here where I am now between Wounded Knee Creek and Grass Creek. Others came too, and we made these little gray houses of logs that you see, and they are square. It is a bad way to live, for there can be no power in a square.

You have noticed that everything an Indian does is in a circle, and that is because the Power of the World always works in circles, and everything tries to be round. In the old days when we were a strong and happy people, all our power came to us from the sacred hoop of the nation, and so long as the hoop was unbroken, the people flourished. The flowering tree was the living center of the hoop, and the circle of the four quarters nourished it. The east gave peace and light, the south gave warmth, the west gave rain, and the north with its cold and mighty wind gave strength and endurance. This knowledge came to us from the outer world with our religion. Everything the Power of the World does is done in a circle. The sky is round, and I have heard that the earth is round like a ball, and so are all the stars. The wind, in its greatest power, whirls. Birds make their nests in circles, for theirs is the same religion as ours. The sun comes forth and goes down again in a circle. The moon does the same, and both are round. Even the seasons form a great circle in their changing, and always come back again to where they were. The life of a man is a circle from childhood to childhood, and so it is in everything where power moves. Our tepees were round like the nests of birds, and these were always set in a circle, the nation's hoop, a nest of many nests, where the Great Spirit meant for us to hatch our children.

But the Wasichus have put us in these square boxes. Our power is gone and we are dying, for the power is not in us any more. You can look at our boys and see how it is with us. When we were living by the power of the circle in the way we should, boys were men at twelve or thirteen years of age. But now it takes them very much longer to mature. . . .

A New Value of Pi

Mathematicians are still trying to calculate the exact value of pi, *but Harvey Carter offers an easier solution in his poem.*

'Tis a favorite project of mine
A new value of *pi* to assign.
    I would fix it at 3
    For it's simpler, you see,
Than 3 point 1 4 1 5 9.

Harvey L. Carter

Checkers

BY MYRA COHN LIVINGSTON

As Myra Cohn Livingston points out in her poem, probabilities can change — with a little practice!

What if
every time
you came
we would play the same old game
and the score was just the same?

I'd win one
and you'd win three.
That is how it seems to be
but for the
probability

that if
I figure out a way
and find some better moves to play
why —
I'll be beating you one day!

Shall I Consider You

BY LILLIAN MORRISON

In addition to using Lillian Morrison's poem as an introduction to integers, you may wish to extend it to a science activity.

a plus or minus?
or plus and minus
to cancel each other out
and make zero? Let's say
negative and positive,
the essential electrical charge
that makes sparks fly,
cells die, and changes
the world every second.

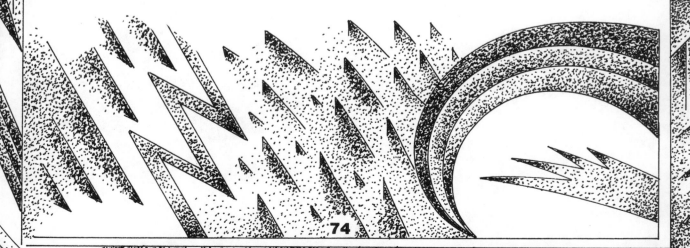

MATH CONNECTION
Problem Solving

CULTURAL CONNECTION
Folktale from Africa

Crossing the River

FROM Stories to Solve, Folktales from Around the World
TOLD BY GEORGE SHANNON

Faced with the same predicament, how would your students solve the problem of transporting themselves, a wolf, a goat, and a cabbage across a river in a very small boat?

Once there was a man who had to take a wolf, a goat, and a cabbage across a river. But his boat was so small it could hold only himself and one other thing. The man didn't know what to do. How could he take the wolf, the goat, and the cabbage over one at a time, so that the wolf wouldn't eat the goat and the goat wouldn't eat the cabbage?

HOW IT WAS DONE
Solution 1

He could take the goat over and go back alone. Then take the wolf over and then bring the goat back. Then take the cabbage over and leave the goat behind. And finally make one last trip and take the goat over to join the wolf and cabbage.

Solution 2

He could take the goat over and go back alone. Then take the cabbage over and bring the goat back. Then take the wolf over and leave the goat behind. And finally go back and get the goat on the last trip.

INDEX

•INDEX BY TITLE•

•INDEX OF MATH CONNECTIONS•

•INDEX BY CATEGORY•

•INDEX BY AUTHOR•

•INDEX OF SELECTIONS BY CONTINENT•

ACKNOWLEDGMENTS *(continued)*

Excerpts from HOMER PRICE by Robert McCloskey. Copyright 1943 by Robert McCloskey, renewed © 1971 by Robert McCloskey. Used by permission of Viking Penguin, a division of Penguin Books USA Inc.

Excerpt from ERIN MCEWAN, YOUR DAYS ARE NUMBERED by Alan Ritchie. Copyright © 1990 by Alan Ritchie. Reprinted by permission of Alfred A. Knopf, Inc.

Excerpt pp. 100–103 from "King Kaid of India" from The Victorian Readers, Fifth Book. Reprinted by permission of Department of Education, Victoria, Australia.

"The Roads of Math" by Jeffrey Dielle is from THE ARITHMETIC TEACHER. Copyright by The National Council of Teachers of Mathematics. Reprinted with permission of The National Council of Teachers of Mathematics.

"Laying Out a Capital City" from BENJAMIN BANNEKER: GENIUS OF EARLY AMERICA by Lillie Patterson. Copyright © 1978 by Lillie Patterson. Reprinted by permission of the author.

"Checkers" by Myra Cohn Livingston. Copyright © 1993 by Myra Cohn Livingston. Used by permission of Marian Reiner for the author.

"Mathemagician" by Sandra Liatsos. Copyright © 1993 by Sandra Liatsos. Used by permission of Marian Reiner for the author.

"Life in Flatland" adapted from *Mathemagic*, Volume 13 of CHILDCRAFT- THE HOW AND WHY LIBRARY. 1988 Edition © 1987 World Book, Inc. Reprinted by permission of World Book, Inc.

"La Suerte" from CUENTOS: TALES FROM THE HISPANIC SOUTHWEST by José Griego y Maestas and Rudolfo A. Anaya. Copyright © 1980 by Museum of New Mexico Press. Reprinted with permission of the Museum of New Mexico Press.